RSPB

WHERE TO GO BIRDWATCHING

A GUIDE TO RSPB NATURE RESERVES

RSPB
WHERE TO GO BIRDWATCHING

A GUIDE TO RSPB NATURE RESERVES

FOREWORD BY TONY SOPER

BBC BOOKS

PHOTOGRAPHIC ACKNOWLEDGEMENTS

Agence Nature (NHPA), p. 84; Heather Angel, p. 43; J. A. Bailey (Ardea), pp. 42, 73; Dr Alan Beaumont, p. 118; Frank V. Blackburn, p. 109; A. C. Clay (RSPB), pp. 18, 20, 26, 32, 47, 55, 64; D. N. Dalton (NHPA), p. 75; Stephen Dalton (NHPA), pp. 36, 71; L. R. Dawson (Bruce Coleman Ltd), p. 54; Gerald Downey, p. 21; D. Dugan (Frank W. Lane), p. 52; Ernest Duscher (Bruce Coleman Ltd), p. 68; C. H. Gomersall (RSPB), pp. 13, 15, 27, 31, 33, 39, 40, 41, 48, 50, 57, 65, 70, 74, 77, 85, 87, 89, 91, 96, 97, 103, 106, 108, 110, 113, 117, 119, 120, 123; M. J. Gore, p. 14; Dennis Green, pp. 82, 88, 92, 98 (Bruce Coleman Ltd), 105; John Hawkins (E. & D. Hosking), p. 93; E. & D. Hosking, pp. 19, 37, 59, 61, 94, 107; John Humphrey, p. 111; Bjorn Huseby (Aquila), p. 125; S. Jonasson (Frank W. Lane), p. 79; M. King & M. Read, p. 121; Chris Knights (Ardea), p. 25; Peter Lamb (Ardea), p. 101; Gordon Langsbury, pp. 95, 115 (Bruce Coleman Ltd); Michael Leach, p. 124; R. T. Mills (Aquila), pp. 29, 35; G. P. Mudge, p. 62; W. S. Paton (Aquila), p. 99; Hans Reinhard (Bruce Coleman Ltd), p. 16; Michael W. Richards (RSPB), pp. 2, 6, 28, 30, 44, 56, 67, 72; John Robinson, p. 22; RSPB, pp. 34, 51; Alistair Smith, p. 122; Roger Tidman, pp. 17, 104 (Nature Photographers); D. & K. Urry, pp. 53 (Bruce Coleman Ltd), 112 (Ardea); Richard Vaughan (Ardea), p. 80; M. C. Wilkes (Aquila), p. 23; Roger Wilmshurst (Bruce Coleman Ltd), pp. 24, 49, 63, 69; Martin B. Withers (Frank W. Lane), p. 100.

All the photographs were supplied through the RSPB.

Jacket illustration Greenland barnacle geese on the island of Islay in the Hebrides. In 1984 the RSPB bought 3000 acres of farmland on Loch Gruinart on Islay (page 91) to manage it particularly for the wintering geese.
Photograph by C. H. Gomersall (RSPB)

Frontispiece The chalk cliffs at Bempton, Humberside (page 18), the largest seabird breeding colony in England.

Great care has been taken throughout this book to ensure accuracy but the Society cannot accept responsibility for any error that may have occurred.

Edited by Anthony Chapman
Maps by Hilary Welch

Published by BBC Books,
a division of BBC Enterprises Limited
Woodlands, 80 Wood Lane, London W12 0TT

ISBN 0 563 20777 9

Typeset in ITC Garamond 9/10pt by
Ace Filmsetting Ltd, Frome, Somerset
Colour separations by Dot Gradations Ltd, Chelmsford
Printed in Great Britain by Cambus Litho, East Kilbride
Bound in Great Britain by Hunter & Foulis Ltd, Edinburgh
Cover printed by Fletchers of Norwich

CONTENTS

FOREWORD

The hidden strength of the RSPB is that, in working for birds, it is actually promoting a healthy environment for everything from worms, to you and me. The network of RSPB reserves is living proof of the diversity and natural beauty which can flourish when enlightened management tills the land. For, as any reserve warden will tell you, a certain amount of honest sweat is involved.

RSPB reserves offer rippling streams, oakwoods and gannet islands in Wales, flower-bedecked flood meadows in West Sedgemoor, stunning mountains, moorlands and pine forests in Scotland, goose grounds and wader lagoons in East Anglia and much, much more. And not all of the reserves are out in the wilds; some explore the living potential of cities and take delight in opening children's eyes to the beauty and fascination of birds.

A hundred years ago, the newly-hatched Society aimed to preserve attractive birds from extinction. It soon learnt that it wasn't enough simply to stop people shooting egrets and trapping kingfishers to fuel the fashion for absurd hats and ballgowns. And it wasn't enough to put a stout fence round a bird's nest and put up a fierce notice saying 'keep out'. So the concept of bird reserves took root and flourished. For it is a waste of time to give a bird legal protection if it has nothing to eat and nowhere to rest and nest. Avocets need salty lagoons well stocked with shrimps; ospreys need healthy fishing lakes and undisturbed trees to nest in. Some will say that the only function of a landscape is to maximise its barley-yield, but half a million members of the RSPB know that a healthy variety of life-forms offers us more interest today and a somewhat improved chance of survival tomorrow.

RSPB reserves are great places to visit, they nurture wonderful birds and add to the joys of life. On top of all that, they act as a shining beacon leading to the inescapable conclusion that this is the way most landscapes ought to be. They are oases bursting with life in a desert of dreary uniformity. Sooner or later the seed will germinate and the whole of Britain will blossom into a giant nature reserve. We can all make a start in the garden, planting berry-bearing shrubs, native trees and our very own grassy sward. But in becoming members of the most effective conservation organisation in the world we make a powerful contribution to a saner planet.

Each and every reserve described in this book has its own special flavour, and each one is watched over by people who care intensely for its maintenance. Go to see them and enjoy their treasures. If you're not yet a member, sample the wares and we warmly welcome you to join us. If you're already a member, please think of a way of contributing a bit more to further the mighty work. As a long-time supporter I am fortunate enough to know many of the Society's professionals. In admiring their dedication I know how much they rely on our appreciation and practical support.

Tony Soper
January 1989

Ouse Washes, Cambridgeshire

VISITING RSPB RESERVES

The Royal Society for the Protection of Birds has a long tradition of establishing nature reserves, starting with the bird sanctuaries of pre-war years and building up to the present total of 115 reserves which are located throughout the United Kingdom. A large body of reserve wardens, backed up by a team of managers, land agents and ecologists, ensure that the RSPB's land-holding is managed to the best advantage of wild bird populations and other native wildlife. The Society's accumulated experience in practical habitat management for nature conservation is second to none.

In fulfilment of the objective, expressed by the Society's Royal Charter, of 'developing a public interest in wild birds and their place in nature', most of our reserves have the facilities to enable a lot of visitors to enjoy them for their scenery, their pleasant walks and, above all, their exciting variety of wild birds. RSPB reserve habitats range from rolling moorland to wide estuaries, from spectacular sea-cliffs to quiet marshes and from broad-leaved woodlands to precious heaths.

Our policy is to encourage RSPB and Young Ornithologists' Club members, as well as the general public, to visit our reserves, subject only to the restrictions that must be applied to fulfil their main purpose – to provide rich and undisturbed places for wild birds to use for nesting, feeding, roosting and as resting-places on migration. Other scientific features must also be conserved with care.

By providing wardening, both paid and voluntary, and installing nature trails and waymarked paths, boardwalks, observation hides and information centres, we can reconcile the twin objectives of bird conservation and showing birds to people – a special technique that the RSPB has developed over two decades of imaginative reserve management.

This guide has been produced with the aim of helping more people to enjoy the reserves whose survival depends on the support of over half a million RSPB and YOC members as well as the goodwill of all those who visit them.

We hope that you will enjoy visiting many of these RSPB reserves.

ENQUIRIES

RSPB offices to which enquiries should be made:

Reserves Division, The Royal Society for the Protection of Birds, The Lodge, Sandy, Bedfordshire SG19 2DL (tel: 0767 80551).

RSPB Scottish Headquarters, 17 Regent Terrace, Edinburgh EH7 5BN (tel: 031 556 5624).

RSPB Wales Office, Bryn Aderyn, The Bank, Newtown, Powys SY16 2AB (tel: 0686 626678).

RSPB Northern Ireland Office, Belvoir Park Forest, Belfast BT8 4QT (tel: 0232 491547).

RSPB North of England Office, 'E' Floor, Milburn House, Dean Street, Newcastle upon Tyne NE1 1LE (tel: 091 232 4148).

RSPB South-East England Office, 8 Church Street, Shoreham-by-Sea, West Sussex BN4 5DQ (tel: 0273 463642).

RSPB South-West England Office, 10 Richmond Road, Exeter EX4 4JA (tel: 0392 432691).

RSPB Orkney Officer, Smyril, Stenness, Stromness KW16 3JX (tel: 0856 850176).

RSPB Shetland Officer, Seaview, Sandwick ZE2 9HP (tel: 095 05 506).

RSPB RESERVES

Lumbister
Fetlar
Loch of Spiggie

Noup Cliffs
North Hill
Marwick Head
Trumland
The Loons
Birsay/Cottasgarth
North Hoy
Hobbister
Copinsay

Handa

Balranald

Culbin Sands
Loch of Strathbeg

Loch Ruthven
Loch Garten
Insh Marshes

Fowlsheugh

Killiecrankie
Loch of Kinnordy

Inversnaid
Vane Farm

Loch Gruinart

Baron's Haugh
Lochwinnoch

Rathlin Island Cliffs
Lough Foyle

Coquet Island

Wood of Cree
Ken-Dee Marshes

Shanes Castle

Geltsdale

Campfield Marsh

Castlecaldwell Forest

Mull of Galloway

Haweswater

Green Island & Greencastle Point

St Bees Head
Hodbarrow
Leighton Moss & Morecambe Bay

Bempton Cliffs

Hornsea Mere

Fairburn Ings

South Stack Cliffs
Point of Air
Gayton Sands
Valley Lakes

Eastwood

Blacktoft Sands
Tetney Marshes

Coombes Valley & Churnet Valley Woods

Titchwell Marsh

Lake Vyrnwy
Mawddach Valley
Ynys-hir
Dyffryn Wood

Frampton Marshes
Snettisham
Strumpshaw Fen & Surlingham Church Marsh
Berney Marshes

Sandwell Valley
Nene Washes
Ouse Washes

Minsmere
North Warren
Havergate Island

Dinas & Gwenffrwd
The Lodge
Fowlmere
Wolves Wood

Highnam Woods
Nagshead

Grassholm

Cwm Clydach

Rye House Marsh
Stour Wood & Copperas Bay
Old Hall Marshes

Church Wood
Northward Hill
Nor Marsh & Motney Hill
Elmley Marshes

Chapel Wood
West Sedgemoor

Barfold Copse
Church Wood, Blean
Tudeley Woods

Garston Wood
Fore Wood
Dungeness

Aylesbeare Common
Langstone Harbour
Adur Estuary

Exminster Marshes
Arne
Pilsey Island
Radipole & Lodmoor

50 km
50 miles

9

VISITING ARRANGEMENTS

The arrangements for visiting each of the reserves described in this guide are expected to remain, but the RSPB reserves the right to modify them if necessary. The current arrangements for each year are given in a free *Reserves Visiting* leaflet which is issued to members with the winter issue of the Society's quarterly magazine *Birds*, or is obtainable free from RSPB headquarters. Visitor facilities are being improved year by year.

All visitors to our reserves are asked to observe the following **standard rules**:

In many cases only *part* of the reserve is open to visitors, the remainder being kept quiet for the wildlife or closed for management reasons. Information Centres, shops, and in some cases hides and toilets, are *not necessarily* open all the hours that the particular reserve is.

Entry charges (where indicated) are incurred by non-members only, and children are admitted at half-price. Members of the RSPB and YOC (including those covered by supplements) are admitted *free* on production of their *membership cards*. We regret that charges cannot be refunded. Both members and non-members are sometimes charged for additional services (e.g. boat trips and escorted walks).

Coach parties and groups of ten or more people must arrange their visit *well in advance* by writing (enclosing a stamped addressed envelope) to the warden, who may be able to escort them.

Dogs may not be taken into the reserves.

Visitors may encounter management necessarily being undertaken in a part of the reserve which may involve temporary disturbance to the birds. We regret any inconvenience that may be caused in these circumstances.

General enquiries to the Reserves Division, RSPB, The Lodge, Sandy, Bedfordshire SG19 2DL (tel: 0767 80551).

ADDITIONAL NOTES

Tenure The RSPB either owns the land for its reserves or leases it from one or more owners. Sometimes the reserve is established by management agreement with the owner. Reserves are being extended all the time, so the acreage and boundary indicated may not be up-to-date in each case.

Status A Site of Special Scientific Interest (**SSSI**) is land which is officially classified by the Nature Conservancy Council as being of particular importance for nature conservation, under the provisions of the Wildlife and Countryside Act, 1981. (A different system operates in Northern Ireland.) **Grades 1 or 2** refer to those sites which are listed in *A Nature Conservation Review* – the NCC's inventory of élite nature conservation land in Britain. An asterisk indicates that a site has international importance. Some reserve wetlands are of international importance for wildfowl and waders through being designated under the **Ramsar** Convention on Wetlands of International Importance especially as Waterfowl Habitat. **SPA** indicates sites that are designated as Special Protection Areas under the provisions of the EEC Directive on the Conservation of Wild Birds.

Birds The information is necessarily brief and selective but is intended to convey the ornithological 'flavour' of each reserve during the breeding season and at other times of the year. All the species mentioned will not necessarily be present during a particular visit.

Other wildlife A few notable species of flora and fauna which may be encountered by the visitor are given to enhance the interest of the reserve.

PRACTICAL POINTS FOR VISITORS

Look for this sign! Special RSPB road **Direction Signs** are being erected over a period of time throughout the country to guide travellers to the reserves.

Shading indicates the **Reserve Area**, but in some cases it has not been possible to include the entire holding on these maps.

→ The directions under **Location**, coupled with the map, are intended to guide visitors, with the aid of an OS map or road atlas, to the **Reserve Entrance** or other access points. The national six-figure grid reference usually refers to that point.

P Reserve (or nearby) **Car Park**. The words 'car parking' indicate informal and limited space for parking such as in a lay-by.

& Some facilities for **Disabled Visitors**. We try to make it possible for disabled people to visit and enjoy our reserves for birdwatching wherever practicable. In many instances hides have been adapted for wheelchair access and in others special paths and boardwalks have been installed. A *free* leaflet with further details of disabled access is available from the Reserves Division.

i Visitors are referred to the local **Tourist Information Centre**, which can advise about local accommodation, bus and rail services etc. The larger ones can book accommodation for visitors. The Society does not maintain details of accommodation near the reserves, but a large number of hotels, guest houses and bed and breakfast addresses near to RSPB reserves advertise in *Birds*, the Society's membership magazine.

C Many reserves are equipped with some form of **Information Centre**, ranging from Nature Centres, with their teaching facilities and shops, to outdoor shelters with identification displays and basic reserve guidance. *Please note* that these buildings are not necessarily open all the hours that the particular reserve is.

G **Guide** A series of illustrated leaflets or booklets, describing individual reserves more fully, are for sale on reserves or by post (adding 20p to the price indicated) from RSPB headquarters.

S Several reserves have a **Shop** that sells items from the RSPB gift catalogue.

WC **Toilets** are available on or beside the reserve.

Public transport For those who choose to visit our reserves by public transport, the nearest British Rail station is listed in each case. Occasionally the station is within walking distance, but usually a bus or taxi will be needed to complete the journey to the reserve.

Clothing and footwear Visitors are advised to wear or carry warm and waterproof garments because the weather on reserves, particularly those in upland or exposed situations, can be inclement, even in summer. Visitor paths are often uneven, sometimes rugged, so stout shoes or boots should be worn. Wellingtons are advisable for wet habitats like the marshes.

Wardens Bearing in mind their other duties, wardens or their assistants are pleased to answer written enquiries and to advise visitors on arrival as to where to go and which birds are about. Please note the requirement under *Standard Rules* for group visits.

Nature trails Some are interpreted with leaflets, others with path-side display boards. In other cases, simple **waymarked paths** are provided.

Refreshments We regret that refreshments are generally not available on reserves. However, picnic areas are often provided for visitors to enjoy their own provisions.

HOW TO SEE MORE BIRDS

'When I was warden on the Ouse Washes I would often be sitting in the hide quietly watching the ducks feeding nearby. Then a coach or group of cars would arrive in the car park. As the birdwatchers disgorge from the vehicles, all chatting away, the ducks start to swim gently out from the bankside away from the hides. The birdwatchers come along the path and noisily cross the bridge over the river; the ducks swim faster. Finally, the visitors stamp up the steps and the straggling ducks take off. So by the time the watchers are in the hides there are no ducks nearer than half a mile. Then there is always the chap who, because the hide is crammed with people, has to stand on top of the bank silhouetted against the fine fenland sky! That is the last straw for the ducks: they go, and they have 20 miles to choose from.'

Jeremy Sorensen, RSPB Warden
(*Birds* magazine, 1983)

The lesson is obvious: be quiet, careful and inconspicuous. Choose subdued colours for clothes and wear a hat of some sort – to disguise head shape. Walk quietly and slowly, do not talk loudly, make use of cover such as banks, trees and bushes. Avoid the skyline and try to keep the light behind you. In many areas, especially woodland, it pays to find a sheltered spot, perhaps on the edge of a clearing or ride, sit still and let the birds come to you.

When watching birds at sea, choose a time of day when the sun is behind you. Pick a viewpoint that juts out over the sea: about 20–30 feet above sea level. Remember that birds sitting on the water are in the valleys of the swell most of the time, so pan very slowly to give yourself a good chance of seeing them.

In a hide, to avoid disturbing the birds, open and close doors and windows quietly; close the flaps before you leave; do not put your hands or binoculars through the viewing holes.

BIRDWATCHERS' CODE OF CONDUCT

Today's birdwatchers are a powerful force for nature conservation. The number of those of us interested in birds rises continually and it is vital that we take seriously our responsibility to avoid any harm to birds. We must also present a responsible image to non-birdwatchers who may be affected by our activities and particularly those on whose sympathy and support the future of birds may rest.

There are 10 points to bear in mind:

1. The welfare of birds must come first.

2. Habitat must be protected.

3. Keep disturbance to birds and their habitat to a minimum.

4. When you find a rare bird think carefully about whom you should tell.

5. Do not harass rare migrants.

6. Abide by the bird protection laws at all times.

7. Respect the rights of landowners.

8. Respect the rights of other people in the countryside.

9. Make your records available to the local bird recorder.

10. Behave abroad as you would when birdwatching at home.

Haweswater, Cumbria

RSPB
RESERVES
IN ENGLAND

ADUR ESTUARY, WEST SUSSEX

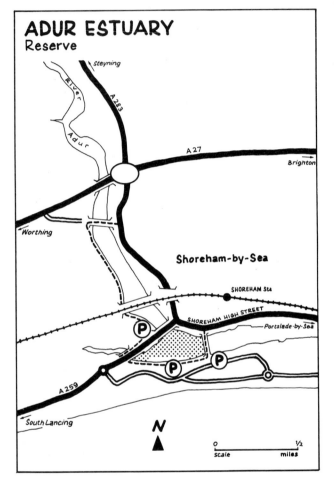

ADUR ESTUARY Reserve

BIRDS Redshank, ringed plover and dunlin feed in winter on the mud, roosting at high tides on the nearby airfield. Avocet, bar-tailed godwit, curlew, whimbrel, knot and shelduck are occasionally seen. Several gull species occur including rare sightings of the Mediterranean gull.

OTHER WILDLIFE Sea purslane, glasswort and sea aster are some of the saltwater plants.

VISITING Good views may be obtained of the river from adjacent footpaths near Shoreham High Street. An illustrated leaflet *River Adur Wildlife Walk* is available (price 20p) from the RSPB South-East England Office (page 8). There is a car park at the edge of the recreation ground by Norfolk Bridge (TQ/211050).

FACILITIES P

i 86 High Street, Shoreham-by-Sea, West Sussex (tel: 079 17 2086).

NEAREST RAILWAY STATION Shoreham (¼ mile).

Redshank

LOCATION Occupying a portion of the tidal River Adur within Shoreham-by-Sea, the reserve may be viewed from the south side between the footbridge from the town centre and the A259 Norfolk Bridge. TQ/211050.

TENURE 25 acres owned.

STATUS SSSI.

WARDEN None present. Enquiries to RSPB South-East England Office (page 8).

HABITAT Inter-tidal mudflats and saltmarsh.

ARNE, DORSET

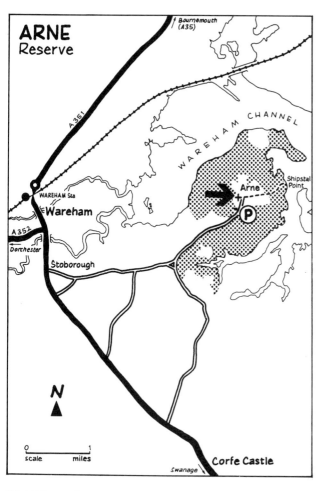

LOCATION The Arne peninsula lies in Poole Harbour east of Wareham, and the reserve is approached off the A351 road to Swanage, ½ mile from Wareham, turning as signposted in Stoborough. SY/473882.

TENURE 1258 acres, mostly owned.

STATUS SSSI. Grade 1*.

WARDEN Bryan Pickess, Syldata, Arne, Wareham BH20 5BJ.

HABITAT Extensive heathland of heather, gorse clumps and scattered pines with some valley bogs. Also mixed woodland, fen with reedbeds and creeks with saltmarsh on the edge of Poole Harbour.

BIRDS Dartford warbler, nightjar and stonechat breed on the heaths, and sparrowhawk and woodpeckers in the woods. Large flocks of black-tailed godwit and spotted redshank use the foreshore during migration. Wintering species include red-breasted merganser, goldeneye, wigeon and hen harrier.

OTHER WILDLIFE Roe and sika deer, all six species of British reptiles including sand lizard and smooth snake, and 22 species of dragonflies which favour the bogs and pools are part of Arne's rich fauna.

VISITING The Shipstal part of the reserve is open at all times, the rest of the reserve being closed except to parties by prior arrangement with the warden. The reserve cark park, with toilets, is situated in Arne village and the public bridleway to Shipstal, with its nature trail and leaflet, starts opposite the church. Visitors are expected to keep to the paths and trackways, except on the beach.

FACILITIES   **P**   **WC**   **G** 50p

i   The Whitehouse, Shore Road, Swanage (tel: 0929 422885).

NEAREST RAILWAY STATION Wareham with connecting bus service through Stoborough (4 miles).

Heather, saltmarsh and reedbeds

AYLESBEARE COMMON, DEVON

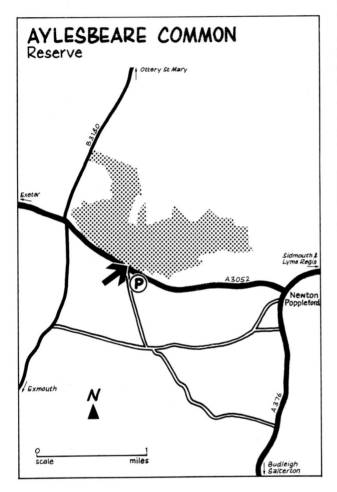

AYLESBEARE COMMON
Reserve

HABITAT Both dry and wet heathland with valley bogs, streams, some woodland and alder scrub.

BIRDS Dartford warbler, nightjar, stonechat, yellowhammer, tree pipit, grasshopper warbler and curlew breed on the heath, and marsh tit and wood warbler in the woodland.

OTHER WILDLIFE Plants include dwarf gorse, pale butterwort, bog pimpernel and royal fern. Roe deer, wood cricket, adder and up to 21 dragonfly species occur. Thirty-eight species of butterfly have been recorded.

VISITING Access at all times, but visitors are asked to keep to the footpaths and firebreak paths from which good views of the reserve are obtained. A waymarked trail starts directly across the road from the public car park.

FACILITIES P

i Silver Street, Ottery St Mary, Devon (tel: 040 481 3964).

NEAREST RAILWAY STATION Exeter (6 miles).

Roe deer

LOCATION Comprising part of the Pebblebed Commons of south Devon, the reserve lies to the north of the A3052 Lyme Regis to Exeter road one mile west of Newton Poppleford. SY/057898.

TENURE 450 acres leased from the Clinton Devon Estates.

STATUS SSSI. Grade 1.

WARDEN Peter Gotham, c/o RSPB South-West England Office (page 8).

BARFOLD COPSE, SURREY

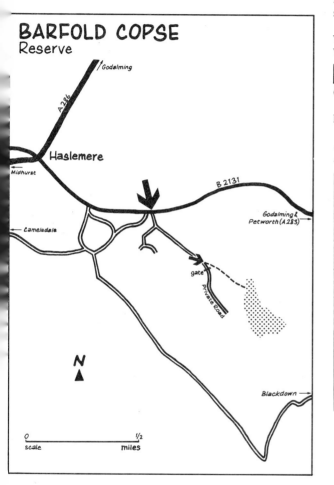

BARFOLD COPSE
Reserve

LOCATION Off the B2131 road to Petworth ½ mile east of Haslemere. Park by the *second* turning to Black Down and follow the public footpath then track to the reserve. SU/914324.

TENURE 13 acres owned.

WARDEN None present. Enquiries to RSPB South-East England Office (page 8).

HABITAT Deciduous woodland of oak, ash and birch with old hazel coppice, being part of a larger wooded area.

BIRDS The common woodland species including tits, robin and nuthatch nest in the wood.

OTHER WILDLIFE The golden-banded dragonfly is often seen and white admiral butterflies are usual. Wild daffodil, golden-scaled fern and pendulous sedge are among the plants.

VISITING Access at all times along the woodland paths. Visitors should keep clear of the derelict buildings.

ℹ️ The Library, 27 The Square, Petersfield, Hampshire (tel: 0730 63451).

NEAREST RAILWAY STATION Haslemere (1 mile).

Nuthatch

BEMPTON CLIFFS, HUMBERSIDE

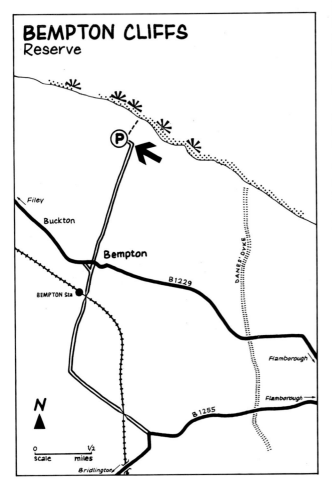

BEMPTON CLIFFS
Reserve

Filey

Buckton

Bempton

BEMPTON Sta

B1229

DANES' DYKE

Flamborough

Flamborough

B1255

N

0   ½
scale   miles

Bridlington

LOCATION Part of the spectacular chalk cliffs that stretch from Flamborough Head to Speeton, the reserve is approached up the cliff road from Bempton village which is on the B1229 from Flamborough, near Bridlington, to Filey. TA/197738.

TENURE Lengths of cliff totalling 2¼ miles are owned.

STATUS SSSI. Grade 1*.

WARDEN Present from April to August, c/o The Post Office, Bempton, near Bridlington, Humberside.

HABITAT Chalk cliffs with numerous cracks and ledges, rising to 400ft in places, and topped by a clay soil with grass and scrub.

BIRDS Enormous numbers of seabirds nest on the cliffs, including thousands of guillemots, razorbills, puffins, kittiwakes, fulmars, herring gulls and several pairs of shags at the boulder base. Here the only gannetry on the mainland of Britain is growing annually, with 810 pairs in 1988. Many migrants pass offshore, including terns, skuas and shearwaters, while species such as wheatear, ring ouzel, merlin and bluethroat frequent the cliff-top on migration.

OTHER WILDLIFE Greater knapweed and pyramidal orchid flower at the cliff-top. Grey seal and porpoise are sometimes seen offshore.

VISITING Access at all times to the cliff-top path on which are sited five safe observation barriers (one on a neighbour's land), providing excellent views of the seabird colonies including the gannetry. Visitors *must* keep to the footpath and observation points because the cliffs are dangerous.

FACILITIES      P   IC   &   G 50p

i Prince Street, Bridlington, Humberside (tel: 0262 673474).

NEAREST RAILWAY STATION Bempton (1½ miles).

The cliffs at Bempton, the highest chalk cliffs in Britain

BERNEY MARSHES, NORFOLK

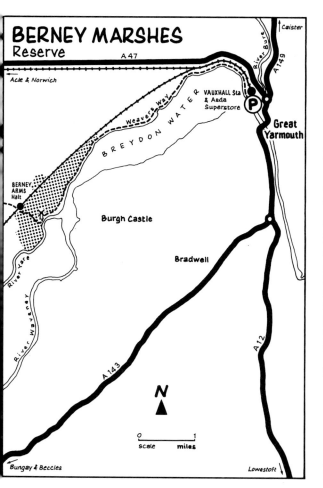

BERNEY MARSHES
Reserve

LOCATION Forming part of the flat, open landscape of the Broadland grazing marshes near Great Yarmouth, the reserve is situated at the confluence of the rivers Yare and Waveney beside Breydon Water. TG/465055.

TENURE 365 acres owned.

WARDEN Les Street, 18 Oaklands Close, Halvergate, Norwich NR13 3PP.

HABITAT Grazing marshes and dykes.

BIRDS Artificial flooding has attracted wintering flocks of wigeon, teal, pintail, mallard and shelduck, as well as brent and white-fronted geese and Bewick's swans occasionally. Shoveler, gadwall, redshank and snipe nest in the marshes which have been visited by ruff, avocet and spoonbill.

OTHER WILDLIFE The dykes contain an interesting flora and abundant invertebrates including the Norfolk aeshna dragonfly.

VISITING No road access, but the railway from Yarmouth and Reedham stops at Berney Arms Halt. The Weaver's Way footpath crosses the reserve from Halvergate or Wickhampton (2 miles) or Yarmouth (4 miles). Boat trips to the reserve are available from Breydon Marine by booking *by post* (enclosing SAE) with the warden: depart *Sundays* 10.00am and 2.00pm. Charge: non-members £2, members £1.

i Marine Parade, Great Yarmouth NR30 2EJ (tel: 0493 842195).

NEAREST RAILWAY STATION Berney Arms Halt (adjacent).

Wigeon

BLACKTOFT SANDS, HUMBERSIDE

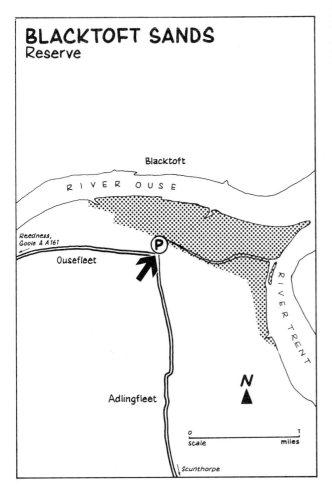

BLACKTOFT SANDS
Reserve

Blacktoft

RIVER OUSE

Reedness,
Goole & A161

Ousefleet

RIVER TRENT

Adlingfleet

N

0   scale   1   miles

Scunthorpe

LOCATION Situated at the confluence of the rivers Ouse and Trent on the inner Humber estuary, the reserve is reached from the A161 road east of Goole through Reedness and Ousefleet. SE/843232.

TENURE 460 acres leased from Associated British Ports.

STATUS SSSI. Grade 1*.

WARDEN Andrew Grieve, Hillcrest, High Street, Whitgift, Goole DN14 8HL.

HABITAT A large tidal reedbed, fringed by saltmarsh, with an area of shallow, brackish water lagoons created by management.

BIRDS Great crested grebe, shoveler, gadwall, pochard and little ringed plover nest on the lagoons which are visited by many species of waders on passage – avocet, stints, greenshank, spotted redshank, godwits, sandpipers and occasional rarities. The reedbeds contain reed and grasshopper warblers, bearded tit and water rail, and a pair of marsh harriers has occasionally nested in them. Short-eared owl, hen harrier and merlin visit in winter as do many wildfowl.

OTHER WILDLIFE Water vole, harvest mouse and fox are present.

VISITING Open on all days *except Tuesday*, 9.00am to 9.00pm or sunset when earlier. £2 charge for non-members. Six hides overlook the lagoons and reeds and are approached from the car park and picnic site by firm paths.

FACILITIES  **P WC IC**   **G** 30p

Goole Library, Carlisle Street, Goole, Humberside (tel: 0405 2187).

NEAREST RAILWAY STATION Goole (8 miles).

Aerial view of the sands

CAMPFIELD MARSH, CUMBRIA

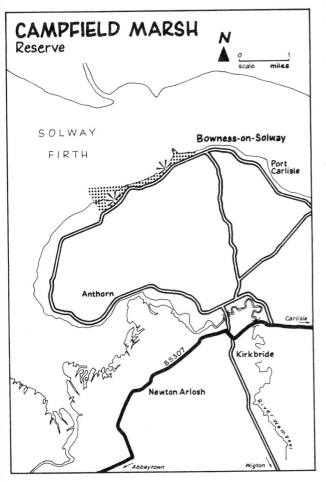

CAMPFIELD MARSH
Reserve

SOLWAY FIRTH

Bowness-on-Solway

Port Carlisle

Anthorn

Carlisle

B5307

Kirkbride

Newton Arlosh

River Wampool

Abbeytown

Wigton

LOCATION Forming part of the southern shore of the Solway estuary, Campfield Marsh is overlooked from the minor road west of Bowness-on-Solway which is reached by the B5307 road from Carlisle through Kirkbride. NY/207620.

TENURE 200 acres owned.

STATUS SSSI. Grade 1*.

WARDEN John Day, 7 Naddlegate, Burn Banks, Haweswater, Penrith CA10 2RL.

HABITAT Tidal saltmarsh with scrub and grassland.

BIRDS The saltings hold big wader roosts at high tides including oystercatcher, knot, curlew, dunlin, lapwing, grey plover and bar-tailed godwit. Further out on the Solway large flocks of duck including mallard, teal, wigeon, pintail, shoveler and scaup occur in winter as well as divers and grebes. In late winter golden plover and pink-footed geese feed on the marsh over which peregrine, sparrowhawk and barn owl may be seen hunting.

OTHER WILDLIFE Typical saltmarsh plants and a colony of northern marsh orchids.

VISITING Good views may be obtained of the high-tide roosts from the roadside lay-bys. *Please do not go onto the marsh.*

FACILITIES **P**

i Town Hall, Green Market, Carlisle CA3 8JH (tel: 0228 25517).

NEAREST RAILWAY STATION Carlisle (12 miles).

Bar-tailed godwit

CHAPEL WOOD, DEVON

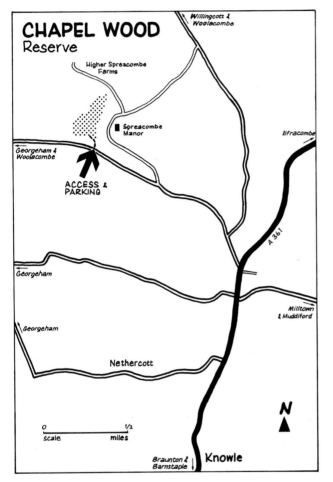

CHAPEL WOOD
Reserve

Willingcott & Woolacombe

Higher Spreacombe Farms

Spreacombe Manor

Ilfracombe

Georgeham & Woolacombe

ACCESS & PARKING

A 361

Georgeham

Georgeham

Milltown & Muddiford

Nethercott

N

0   ½
scale   miles

Braunton & Barnstaple   Knowle

LOCATION Situated near the north Devon coast, this reserve is approached from the A361 Barnstaple to Ilfracombe road, turning to Spreacombe two miles north of Braunton. SS/483413.

TENURE 14 acres owned.

HONORARY WARDEN Cyril Manning, 8 Chichester Park, Woolacombe, North Devon.

HABITAT A valley woodland of oak, beech and birch.

BIRDS Nuthatch, treecreeper, redstart, marsh tit, pied and spotted flycatchers, all three species of woodpecker and occasionally raven and buzzard nest on or near the reserve. Woodcock, redwing and fieldfare occur in winter; dippers are present all year.

OTHER WILDLIFE Fox, red deer and badger sometimes visit the wood.

VISITING The reserve may be visited at any time by obtaining a permit by post from the honorary warden (enclosing SAE). Cars should be parked on the verge near the entrance stile from which visitors cross a field to the reserve gate with the RSPB sign. The gates must be closed. A path, with several branches, encircles the wood.

i 20 Holland Street, Barnstaple, Devon (tel: 0271 72742).

NEAREST RAILWAY STATION Barnstaple (10 miles).

Male pied flycatcher

CHURCH WOOD, BUCKINGHAMSHIRE

CHURCH WOOD
Reserve

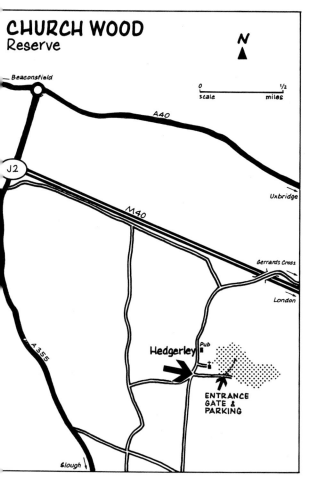

HABITAT Mixed woodland with mature beech, ash and oak as well as birch, alder and hazel coppice, forming part of the more extensive Chiltern woods.

BIRDS Nuthatch, the three species of woodpeckers, stock dove, blackcap and several species of tits nest in this woodland.

OTHER WILDLIFE Fox and muntjac deer occur as do both white admiral and purple hairstreak butterflies. Butcher's broom and green helleborine are interesting plants.

VISITING Access at all times along waymarked paths which encircle the wood. Visitors are asked to park *beside* the track to the field gate and entrance to avoid impeding farm traffic.

i Central Library, St Ives Road, Maidenhead, Berkshire (tel: 0628 781110).

NEAREST RAILWAY STATION Gerrards Cross (4 miles).

Great spotted woodpecker

LOCATION Situated beside the Chilterns village of Hedgerley which is reached from the M40 or A40 intersections near Beaconsfield, turning south on the A355 road to Slough. Immediately south of the M40 turn left for Hedgerley village where a private track to the reserve is entered beside the pond beyond the pub. SU/968873.

TENURE 34 acres owned.

WARDEN None present. Enquiries to RSPB South-East England Office (page 8).

CHURCH WOOD, BLEAN, KENT

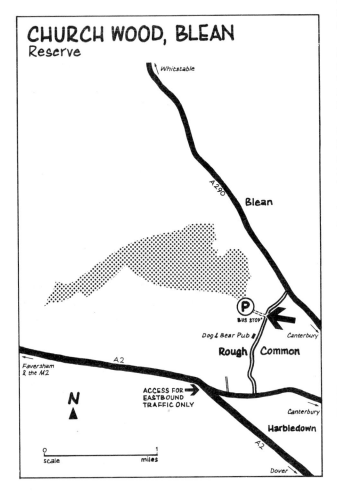

CHURCH WOOD, BLEAN
Reserve

Whitstable

A290

Blean

P
BUS STOP

Dog & Bear Pub

Canterbury

Rough | **Common**

A2

Faversham
& the M2

ACCESS FOR
EASTBOUND
TRAFFIC ONLY

Canterbury

Harbledown

A2

N

Dover

scale   miles
0   1

LOCATION Part of the extensive Blean Forest on the west of Canterbury, Church Wood is entered, as signposted, at Rough Common. Approaching from the west on the A2, take the first road on the left to Canterbury, then the second turning on the left to Rough Common. From Canterbury, take the A290 road to Whitstable, turning after 1½ miles for Rough Common. TR/126593.

TENURE 440 acres owned.

STATUS SSSI. Grade 1.

WARDEN Michael Walter, 11 Garden Close, Rough Common, Canterbury CT2 9BP.

HABITAT Mainly deciduous woodland on clay and gravel soil, being part of a larger block of some 2000 acres. Mature oakwood contrasts with open sweet chestnut coppice and areas of silver birch, and is crossed by several rides.

BIRDS Green, great spotted and lesser spotted woodpeckers, nightingale, tree pipit, willow warbler, blackcap, garden warbler and nuthatch are some of the breeding species, and notably redstart, hawfinch and wood warbler which are scarce in south-east England. Crossbills sometimes occur.

OTHER WILDLIFE One of the few sites of the endangered butterfly, heath fritillary, whose caterpillars feed on the yellow cow-wheat and whose numbers are being increased by habitat management. The butterflies fly on sunny days from mid-June to late July.

VISITING Access at all times along three waymarked paths of one, two and three miles length respectively. Visitors should keep to these paths.

FACILITIES P &

i 34 St Margaret's Street, Canterbury CT1 2TG (tel: 0227 766567).

NEAREST RAILWAY STATION Canterbury East (2 miles).

Nightingale feeding young

CHURNET VALLEY WOODS, STAFFS.

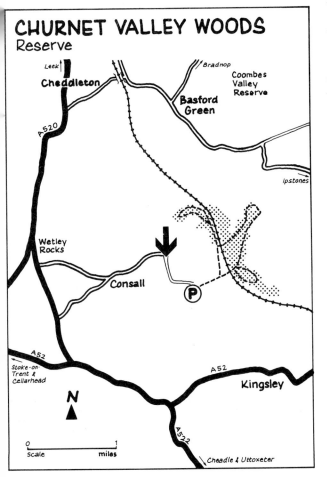

CHURNET VALLEY WOODS
Reserve

BIRDS The resident species of nuthatch, treecreeper, sparrowhawk, tits and woodpeckers are joined in summer by numerous garden warblers, blackcaps, willow warblers, wood warblers and redstarts with several pairs of whitethroat, lesser whitethroat and pied flycatcher. Siskins and redpolls occur in winter.

OTHER WILDLIFE Giant bellflower, broad-leaved helleborine and wild garlic flower in the woodland where white-letter hairstreak butterflies may be seen. Grass snakes are common.

VISITING Access at all times *on foot* from the Country Park car park off the private road (SJ/995483). Visitors should walk downhill to the canal bridge where waymarked paths enter the three woods for circular walks.

FACILITIES   P

i   New Stockwell House, Stockwell Street, Leek, Staffs (tel: 0538 385181).

NEAREST RAILWAY STATION Stoke-on-Trent (13 miles).

Willow warbler

LOCATION Lying in the steep-sided valley of the River Churnet, the three properties of Chase Wood, Rough Knipe and Booths Wood are entered down the minor road from Consall village, east of the A522 from Cheadle to Leek. SS/990489.

TENURE 183 acres owned.

WARDEN Maurice Waterhouse, Coombes Valley Reserve (see page 26).

HABITAT Mature broad-leaved woodland clothing the valley slopes rises to 200ft above the river and canal and contains oak, ash, wych elm, rowan, bird cherry, guelder rose and hazel.

COOMBES VALLEY, STAFFORDSHIRE

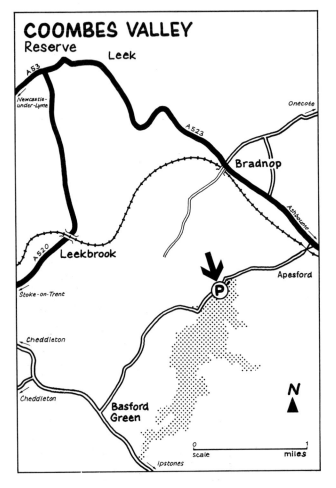

COOMBES VALLEY
Reserve
Leek

LOCATION This secluded valley lies off the A523 road to Ashbourne, three miles south-east of Leek. Turn up the minor road to Apesford (as signposted) and the reserve is entered after one mile. SK/009534.

TENURE 263 acres owned.

STATUS SSSI.

WARDEN Maurice Waterhouse, Six Oaks Farm, Bradnop, Leek ST13 7EU.

HABITAT A steep-sided valley with a rocky stream and slopes covered by oak woodland, bracken clearings and pasture.

BIRDS Redstart, wood warbler and pied flycatcher typify the breeding birds' community which also contains tree pipit, sparrowhawk, tawny and long-eared owls and the three species of woodpeckers. Dipper, grey wagtail and kingfisher frequent the stream. Large flocks of fieldfare, redwing, tits and finches occur in winter.

OTHER WILDLIFE A fine site for badgers which breed in several setts. There is a rich beetle fauna. Several orchid species occur.

VISITING Open on all days *except Tuesday*, 9.00am to 9.00pm or sunset when earlier. £1.50 charge for non-members. A nature trail with leaflet explores the reserve where there are two hides, one overlooking the stream and pond and another elevated in the tree canopy.

FACILITIES   **P**   **WC**   **IC**   **G** 50p

i   New Stockwell House, Stockwell Street, Leek, Staffs (tel: 0538 385181).

NEAREST RAILWAY STATION Stoke-on-Trent (13 miles).

Stream bordered by woodland

COQUET ISLAND, NORTHUMBERLAND

COQUET ISLAND
Reserve

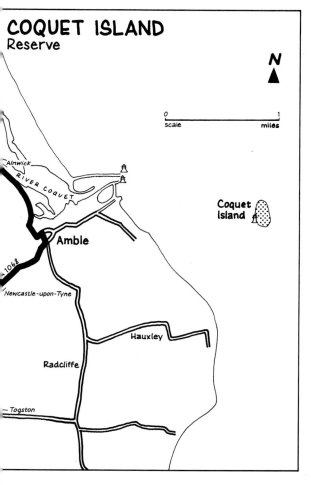

N

HABITAT A low, flat-topped island with rocky and shingle shores.

BIRDS Large colonies of Sandwich, common and Arctic terns nest on the open island as well as several pairs of the scarce roseate tern. Hundreds of puffins breed in turf burrows and there is also a thriving colony of eider ducks.

OTHER WILDLIFE Grey seals, which breed on the Farne Islands to the north, may be seen around the island.

VISITING The RSPB North of England Office arranges seasonal boat trips around the island, weather and tidal conditions permitting. Further information from RSPB North of England Office (page 8).

i Amble Tourist Information Centre, Dilston Terrace, Amble, NE65 0DT (tel: 0665 712313).

NEAREST RAILWAY STATION Acklington (5 miles).

Puffin at Coquet Lighthouse

LOCATION Lying one mile off the Northumberland coast near the village of Amble, this small island may not be visited to avoid disturbing the seabirds. However, a boat trip around it provides good views of the nesting colonies. NU/294046.

TENURE 16 acres leased from the Northumberland Estates.

STATUS SSSI. Grade 2. SPA.

WARDEN Present from April to August, c/o The Post Office, Amble, near Morpeth, Northumberland.

DUNGENESS, KENT

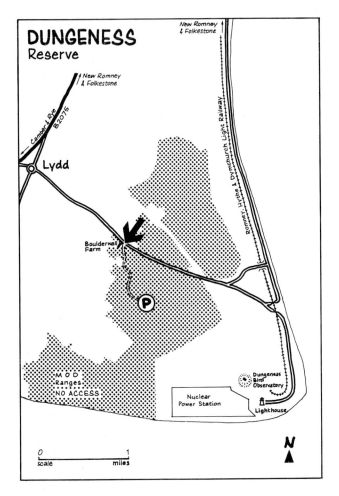

LOCATION Situated on the large and exposed shingle foreland of Dungeness, the reserve is entered off the straight Lydd to Dungeness road as signposted. TR/063196.

TENURE 1260 acres owned with 769 acres leased from Folkestone Water Company.

STATUS SSSI. Grade 1*.

WARDEN Peter Makepeace, Boulderwall Farm, Dungeness Road, Lydd, Romney Marsh, TN29 9PN.

HABITAT Extensive shingle, part of which has been excavated to form flooded pits of high value to waterfowl. Also natural ponds, marshy depressions and scattered clumps of gorse and bramble.

BIRDS The islands of Burrowes Pit have a large nesting colony of common and Sandwich terns with black-headed gulls. Wheatear, great and little grebes also nest. Large flocks of teal, shoveler, mallard, pochard and tufted duck occur outside the breeding season, other winter visitors being goldeneye, goosander, smew and both Slavonian and red-necked grebes. Dungeness is a famous landfall for small migrants including many rarities.

OTHER WILDLIFE The introduced marsh frog is abundant. Viper's bugloss and Nottingham catchfly flower on the shingle.

VISITING Open on all days *except Tuesday*, 9.00am to 9.00pm or sunset when earlier. £2 charge for non-members. Three hides overlook the Burrowes Pit and there is also a waymarked path of 1½ miles length.

FACILITIES **P WC IC** & **G** 50p

 2 Littlestone Road, New Romney, Kent (tel: 0679 64044).

NEAREST RAILWAY STATION Rye (10 miles). A light railway travels from Hythe to Dungeness.

Teasels on the foreshore

EASTWOOD, GREATER MANCHESTER

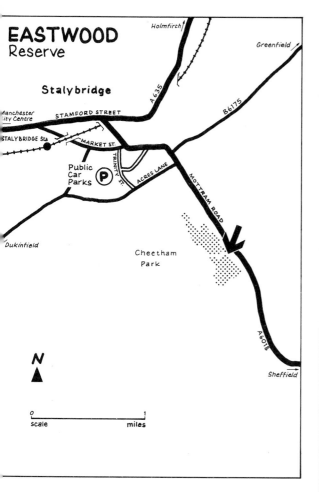

EASTWOOD
Reserve

Stalybridge

Holmfirth

Greenfield

Manchester City Centre

STAMFORD STREET

A635

B6175

STALYBRIDGE Sta.

MARKET ST.

TRINITY ST.

ACRES LANE

MOTTRAM ROAD

Public Car Parks (P)

Dukinfield

Cheetham Park

A6018

Sheffield

N

0   scale   1   miles

LOCATION Lying on the fringe of the Manchester conurbation, this educational reserve is entered from the A6018 road in Stalybridge, beside Cheetham Park, south of its junction with the A635. Public car parks are available in Trinity Street from where visitors should walk to the entrance by the Priory Tennis Club. SJ/972977.

TENURE 12 acres owned.

WARDEN Richard Wakely, 12 Fir Tree Crescent, Dukinfield, SK16 5EH.

HABITAT Broad-leaved woodland of sessile oak, wych elm, ash and beech in a steep-sided valley containing a stream with pools.

BIRDS Grey wagtail, kingfisher and heron frequent the stream and nuthatch, great spotted woodpecker, treecreeper and tawny owl nest in the woodland. Siskin and redpoll may occur in winter and wood warbler and blackcap in summer.

OTHER WILDLIFE Toads, frogs and newts breed in the pools.

VISITING Although primarily intended as an educational reserve with a countryside classroom for schoolchildren, members and the public are welcome to visit it on Saturdays and Sundays throughout the year. School parties are welcome by appointment.

FACILITIES IC

i Town Hall Extension, Lloyd Street, Manchester (tel: 061 234 3157/8).

NEAREST RAILWAY STATION Stalybridge (1 mile).

Grey wagtail

ELMLEY MARSHES, KENT

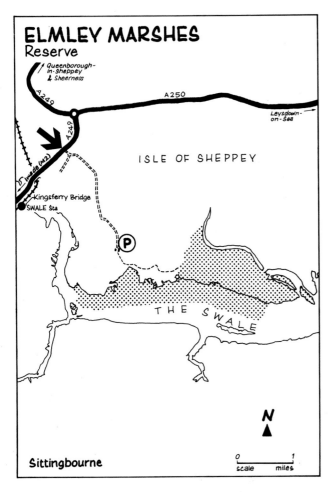

LOCATION Forming part of the extensive North Kent Marshes, the reserve is reached by taking the long farm track which starts from the A249 road to Sheerness one mile beyond Kingsferry bridge. TQ/926705.

TENURE 697 acres leased from Elmley Conservation Trust and the Crown Estate Commissioners.

STATUS SSSI. Grade 1. SPA. Ramsar.

WARDEN Bob Gomes, Kingshill Farm, Elmley, Sheerness, Isle of Sheppey ME12 3RW.

HABITAT Coastal grazing marshes with freshwater fleets and shallow floods, bordered by saltmarsh on the north side of the Swale estuary.

BIRDS Habitat management and wardening has made the Spitend peninsula a major refuge for thousands of wigeon, teal mallard, shelduck and white-fronted geese in winter. The waders include black-tailed godwit, curlew, dunlin and redshank in winter when hen harrier, merlin and short-eared owl occur regularly. In the breeding season redshank, lapwing, pochard, mallard and shoveler are numerous and both avocet and little tern also nest. Curlew sandpiper, spotted redshank and rarities such as Kentish plover use the refuge on passage.

OTHER WILDLIFE A rare moth, the ground lackey, occurs in the saltmarsh. Marsh and common frogs, slow-worm and grass snake are all present.

VISITING Open on all days *except Tuesday*, 9.00am to 9.00pm or sunset if earlier. £1.50 charge for non-members. The Spitend flooded area and saltings are overlooked by five hides which are approached by a mile walk from the reserve car park. (Elderly and disabled visitors are permitted to drive there.) Visitors are asked to keep to the main paths and below the sea-wall to avoid breaking the skyline and disturbing birds.

FACILITIES   P   WC   G 30p

i Bridge Road Car Park, Sheerness, Kent (tel: 0795 665324)

NEAREST RAILWAY STATION Swale (3½ miles).

Freshwater fleet in the Swale estuary

EXMINSTER MARSHES, DEVON

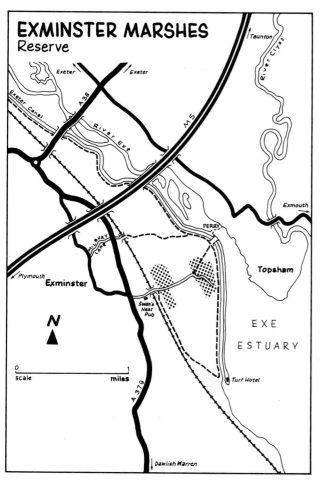

EXMINSTER MARSHES
Reserve

LOCATION Lying at the head of the Exe Estuary, the marshes are approached from the A379 Exeter to Dawlish Warren Road by the village of Exminster. SX/958875.

TENURE 36 acres owned.

STATUS SSSI. Grade 1.

WARDEN Peter Gotham, c/o RSPB South-West England Office (page 8).

HABITAT Coastal grazing marshes with freshwater ditches and shallow floods.

BIRDS Lapwing and redshank breed in the meadows and sedge and reed warblers in the ditches and along the canal. Buzzard and raven occur regularly. Brent geese, wigeon, red-breasted merganser, avocet, black-tailed and bar-tailed godwits, oystercatcher, grey and ringed plovers, curlew, dunlin and turnstone use the adjacent estuary.

OTHER WILDLIFE The ditches are botanically rich including frogbit, flowering rush, water chickweed and several species of duckweed.

VISITING Access at all times. There are no parking facilities at present so visitors are asked to visit *on foot only* along the road leading from the Swan's Nest public house or Milbury Lane in Exminster. Excellent views may be obtained of the estuary and the marshes from this road, the public footpaths and especially by the Turf Hotel.

i Civic Centre, Harris Street, Exeter EX1 1JJ (tel: 0392 265297).

NEAREST RAILWAY STATION Exeter (4 miles).

Brent geese on Bowling Green Marsh in the Exe estuary

FAIRBURN INGS, NORTH YORKSHIRE

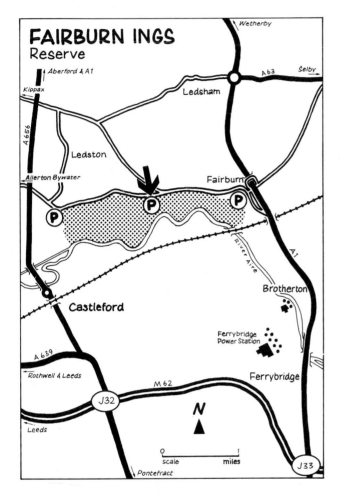

LOCATION Lying immediately west of the A1 north of Ferrybridge, the reserve extends along the Aire valley from the village of Fairburn. SE/452278.

TENURE 680 acres leased from local authorities.

STATUS SSSI. Statutory Bird Sanctuary.

WARDEN Robin Horner, 2 Springholme, Caudle Hill, Fairburn, Knottingley WF11 9JQ.

HABITAT Large shallow lakes, marsh, scrub and flood-pools formed by mining subsidence; deciduous woodland by the river.

BIRDS Of principal importance for wintering wildfowl including mallard, teal, shoveler, pochard, tufted duck, goldeneye, goosander, coot and up to 100 whooper swans. Common, Arctic and black terns, little gull and several wader species occur on passage and both yellow and pied wagtails with swallows gather in large autumnal roosts. Lapwing, redshank, snipe, little ringed plover, common tern, mute swan and both great crested and little grebes nest as do several species of ducks.

OTHER WILDLIFE Interesting marshland plants and dragonflies.

VISITING Access at all times to three public hides overlooking the lakes which are reached via the causeway and footpath below Fairburn village. The reserve information centre with toilets, a raised boardwalk through the marsh (especially suitable for wheelchairs) and a hide beside shallow pools are situated one mile west of the village – open at weekends and Bank holidays throughout the year from 10.00am to 5.00pm. Otherwise good views may be obtained from the road lay-bys. £1 charge for non-members.

FACILITIES   **P**   **WC**   **IC**   &   **G** 30p

 Town Hall, Wood Street, Wakefield, Yorkshire (tel: 0924 370211).

NEAREST RAILWAY STATION Castleford (5 miles).

Ponds and marshland

FORE WOOD, EAST SUSSEX

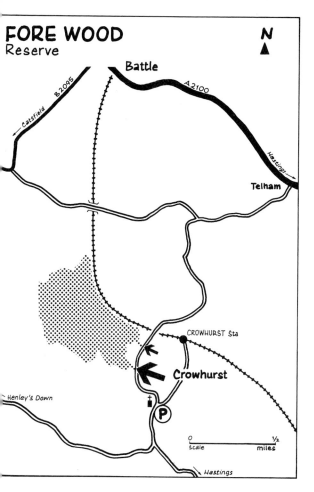

FORE WOOD
Reserve

HABITAT Undulating woodland of coppiced hornbeam and sweet chestnut with oak standards and containing glades, rides, a pond and two ravine (ghyll) streams with waterfalls.

BIRDS There is a growing number of breeding birds due to habitat improvement including great, marsh and willow tits, great and lesser spotted woodpeckers, spotted flycatcher, chiffchaff, garden warbler, nightingale and blackcap. Sparrowhawk and hawfinch occur.

OTHER WILDLIFE Interesting ferns and mosses thrive in the sandstone ghylls. Bluebell, wood anemone and early purple orchid are abundant in spring. White admiral butterflies fly in the rides.

VISITING Access at all times along a nature trail which explores most of the wood. Visitors are asked to park at Crowhurst village hall opposite the church and to walk up the road to either of the reserve entrances.

FACILITIES P

i 88 High Street, Battle, East Sussex (tel: 042 46 3721).

NEAREST RAILWAY STATION Crowhurst (¼ mile).

Deciduous woodland

LOCATION This Wealden woodland lies on the edge of Crowhurst, two miles south-west of Telham on the A2100 Battle – Hastings road. TQ/756126.

TENURE 135 acres owned.

STATUS SSSI.

WARDEN Martin Allison, 2 Hale Farm Cottages, Hart Lake Road, Tudeley, Tonbridge, Kent. An assistant warden is sometimes resident.

FOWLMERE, CAMBRIDGESHIRE

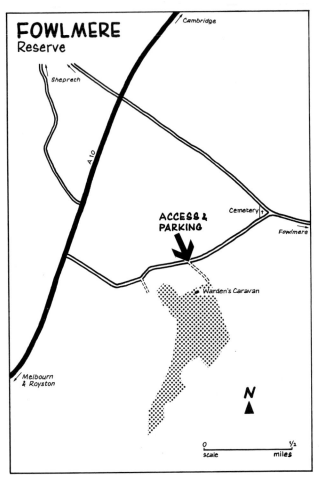

LOCATION Situated near Fowlmere village, the reserve is reached by turning off the A10 Cambridge to Royston road by Shepreth. TL/407461.

TENURE 86 acres owned.

STATUS SSSI.

WARDEN Present from April to August, c/o The Post Office, Fowlmere, Royston SG8 7SU. At other times enquiries to Reserves Division (page 8).

HABITAT An isolated fen within arable farmland comprising reeds and pools fed by spring water; also some hawthorn scrub an alder copse and deciduous woodland.

BIRDS A large colony of reed warblers nest in the reedbeds with sedge warbler, reed bunting, grasshopper warbler and water rail. Kingfishers are seen frequently and green sandpiper occur on migration. Whitethroat and turtle dove nest in the scrub which in autumn and winter is used by large flocks of fieldfare, redwing and corn bunting for roosting with pied wagtails in the reeds.

OTHER WILDLIFE Bee orchid, autumn gentian, field scabiou and cowslip flower in the chalky grass areas. Frogs and toads are abundant in spring.

VISITING Until a proper car park has been provided, cars mu be parked *clear of the entrance track* on the roadside. A nature trail incorporates three hides, one of which is elevated. There is a boardwalk trail for disabled visitors near the entrance.

FACILITIES ♿

i Wheeler Street, Cambridge (tel: 0223 322640).

NEAREST RAILWAY STATION Shepreth (3 miles).

Fen surrounded by farmland

FRAMPTON MARSHES, LINCOLNSHIRE

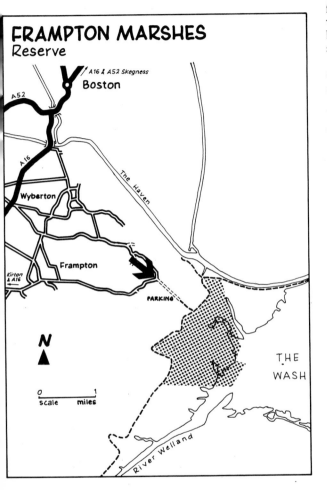

FRAMPTON MARSHES
Reserve

THE WASH

N

River Welland

LOCATION Lying in the south-west corner of The Wash estuary, the reserve is reached by following the signs for Frampton Marsh off the A16 at Kirton. TF/364383.

TENURE 930 acres owned.

STATUS SSSI. Grade 1*. SPA. Ramsar.

WARDEN Present from April to September, c/o The Post Office, Frampton, nr Boston, Lincs. At other times enquiries to Reserves Division (page 8).

HABITAT Mature saltmarsh, partly grazed, leading to a network of creeks and intertidal mudflats.

BIRDS The saltmarsh holds one of the densest concentrations of nesting redshank in Britain. Thousands of brent geese frequent these marshes and flats in winter with shelduck, wigeon and numerous dunlin, knot and redshank. Wintering birds of prey include hen harrier, short-eared owl, sparrowhawk and merlin.

OTHER WILDLIFE Saltmarsh plants including sea aster and sea wormwood.

VISITING Cars may drive down the access track but *must park on the grass verge* out of the way of farm machinery. Good birdwatching may be obtained from the sea-wall but the saltmarsh itself *should not be entered* because of dangerous creeks.

i Stephen Walker Travel, Assembly Rooms, Market Place, Boston PE21 6LY (tel: 0205 56656).

NEAREST RAILWAY STATION Boston (5 miles).

Short-eared owl

GARSTON WOOD, DORSET

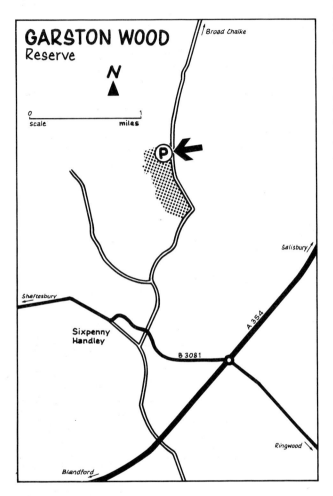

LOCATION Situated on the chalk downs of Cranborne Chase, the reserve is approached from the main Salisbury–Blandford Road one mile north of Sixpenny Handley on the road to Broad Chalke. SU/004194.

TENURE 84 acres owned.

STATUS SSSI. Grade 2.

WARDEN Occasionally present: c/o Arne Reserve (see page 15).

HABITAT Ancient coppice of hazel, field maple and ash with oak standards.

BIRDS Nightingale, turtle dove, garden warbler and yellowhammer nest in the young coppice while marsh tit, nuthatch, great and lesser spotted woodpeckers and buzzard favour the mature woodland. Woodcock, brambling and redpoll occur in winter.

OTHER WILDLIFE The magnificent spring flora include the unusual toothwort, Solomon's seal and both bird's-nest and greater butterfly orchids. White admiral and silver-washed fritillary may be seen along the rides. Roe deer, badger and dormouse are present.

VISITING Access at all times from the small car park along the woodland paths.

FACILITIES   P

ℹ️ Marsh and Ham Car Park, West Street, Blandford DT11 7AW (tel: 0258 51989).

NEAREST RAILWAY STATION Salisbury (15 miles).

Silver-washed fritillary

GAYTON SANDS, CHESHIRE

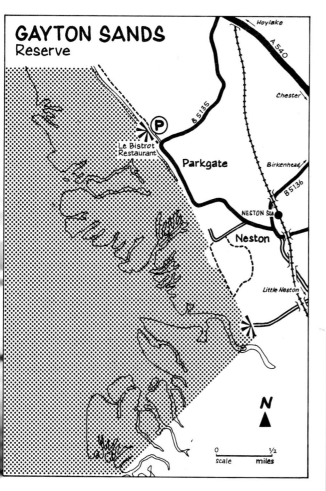

GAYTON SANDS
Reserve

LOCATION Occupying a large part of the east side of the Dee estuary, Gayton Sands is overlooked from Parkgate which is reached from the A540 Chester to Hoylake road via the B5135. SJ/274789.

TENURE 5040 acres owned.

STATUS SSSI. Grade 1*. SPA. Ramsar.

WARDEN Colin Wells, Marsh Cottage, Denhall Lane, Burton, Wirral L64 0TG.

HABITAT Extensive saltmarsh and inter-tidal sandflats, with a reedbed by the shore at Neston.

BIRDS Although shelduck, oystercatcher and redshank nest on the saltmarsh, this reserve is outstanding for its large flocks of pintail, teal, mallard, wigeon and shelduck which frequent the Dee estuary in autumn and winter. Thousands of oystercatcher, grey plover, knot, dunlin, curlew, redshank and bar-tailed godwit assemble on the foreshore where peregrine, merlin and hen harrier often hunt. Twite and brambling often occur.

OTHER WILDLIFE Many moth species occur and noctule bats sometimes hunt over the edge of the saltmarsh.

VISITING Good birdwatching, especially at high tides (times are available from the warden), can be obtained from the Old Baths car park and the adjacent public footpath, located near Le Bistrot Restaurant (SJ/274789). Visitors are advised *not* to venture onto the saltmarsh because of very dangerous tides.

FACILITIES P

i Town Hall, Northgate Street, Chester, Cheshire (tel: 0244 40144).

NEAREST RAILWAY STATION Neston (2 miles).

Shelduck

GELTSDALE, CUMBRIA

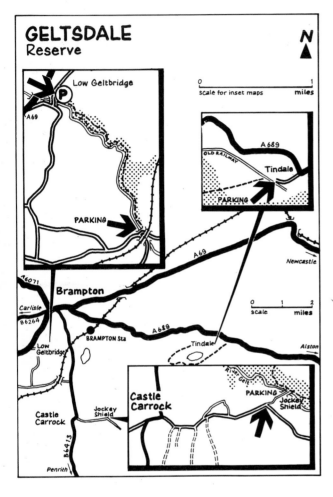

LOCATION Lying within the northern Pennines, the fells of the King's Forest of Geltsdale rise south of the A69 road from Carlisle to Newcastle and may be viewed from the A689 east of Brampton. The reserve also includes several woods in the nearby valleys of the Rivers Gelt and Irthing.

TENURE 12 000 acres of moorland is a reserve by agreement with the owners, while 300 acres of woodland are managed by agreement with several owners.

STATUS The moorland is SSSI, Grade 1. Gelt Woods are SSSI.

WARDEN John Miles, Jockey Shield, Castle Carrock, near Carlisle, Cumbria.

HABITAT Mainly heather moorland rising to the 2000-feet summit of Coldfell, with a tarn and mixed deciduous woodland on steep valley sides.

BIRDS Red grouse, golden plover, curlew, ring ouzel and lapwing nest on the fells and the pastures below them. Large populations of pied flycatcher, redstart, wood warbler and several sparrowhawks breed in the woodland, while the streams hold dipper, grey wagtail, goosander and common sandpiper. Whooper swans and goldeneye visit Tindale Tarn in winter.

OTHER WILDLIFE Some meadows contain globe flower, common wintergreen and bird's-nest orchid. Red squirrels and roe deer inhabit the riverside woods.

VISITING The Geltsdale moorland may be viewed from bridleways starting either at Jockey Shield (NY/561557) east of Castle Carrock or along the old railway line from Tindale off the A689 (NY/616593). A waymarked path runs through the *Lower Gelt Woods*, joining the reserve at Gelt Bridge (NY/520592), with car park, off the A69 from Carlisle 1½ miles south of Brampton, or by the railway viaduct (NY/533573) west of the B6413 road to Castle Carrock three miles south of Brampton – the latter being suitable for wheelchairs.

FACILITIES P ♿

 Moot Hall, Brampton, Cumbria (tel: 069 77 3433).

NEAREST RAILWAY STATION Brampton.

The Black Burn, Geltsdale

HAVERGATE ISLAND, SUFFOLK

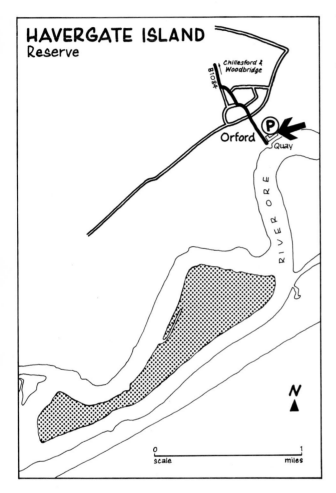

HAVERGATE ISLAND
Reserve

LOCATION Lying within the River Ore on the Suffolk coast, the island is reached by boat from Orford quay. TM/425496.

TENURE 267 acres owned.

STATUS SSSI. Grade 1. SPA. Also part of a National Nature Reserve.

WARDEN John Partridge, 30 Mundays Lane, Orford, Woodbridge IP12 2LX.

HABITAT A low embanked island in the River Ore containing shallow, brackish water lagoons with islands and surrounded by saltmarsh and shingle beaches.

BIRDS Britain's largest nesting colony of avocets was established here in 1947 and now numbers some 120 pairs. Sandwich and common terns, oystercatcher, ringed plover, redshank and shelduck also breed and several wader species occur on passage. Many avocets remain over winter when teal, wigeon, pintail, shoveler, mallard and occasionally Bewick's swan and hen harrier are present.

OTHER WILDLIFE Sea purslane and sea lavender flower on the saltings and sea pea and English stonecrop on the shingle beach. Roesel's bush cricket is a speciality in late summer.

VISITING Boat trips are run to the island between April and August on *Saturdays, Sundays, Mondays* and *Thursdays*, leaving Orford quay at 10.00am and 11.30am. Permits must be obtained by written application *only* from the warden, enclosing SAE for reply (charge: members £2, non-members £3 – payable on arrival). Visiting during September–March is on alternate Thursdays and Saturdays: dates obtainable from the warden. There are several hides as well as an information centre, basic toilets and a picnic area on the island.

FACILITIES **IC G** 30p

i The Cinema, High Street, Aldeburgh, Suffolk (tel: 072 885 3637).

NEAREST RAILWAY STATION Woodbridge (11 miles).

The Saltings

HAWESWATER, CUMBRIA

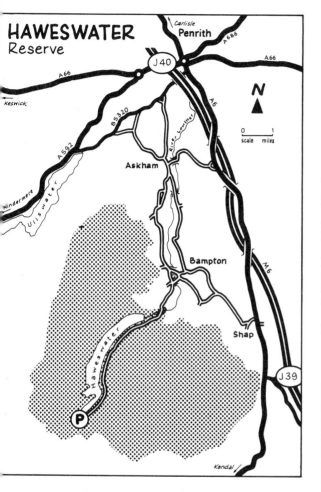

HAWESWATER Reserve

WARDEN John Day, 7 Naddlegate, Burn Banks, near Penrith CA10 2RL.

HABITAT Steep oak and birch woodland surrounded by fells with rocky streams and some heather moor.

BIRDS England's only pair of golden eagles nest on high crags near the head of the reservoir. The other upland breeding species include peregrine, raven, ring ouzel, golden plover, curlew, redshank and snipe while the woodland holds pied flycatcher, wood warbler, tree pipit and redstart as well as buzzard and sparrowhawk.

OTHER WILDLIFE Bird's-eye primrose, lesser twayblade and globe flower are special plants. The woodland is rich in ferns, mosses and lichens. Red squirrels and both roe and red deer may be seen.

VISITING Wardens run an observation post from 8.00am to 6.00pm April–August provided the eagles are nesting – reached by a path from the reservoir car park (NY/469108). Otherwise free access to the fells – but not in the eagle's valley during the breeding season please.

FACILITIES P

i Robinson's School, Middlegate, Penrith CA11 7PT (tel: 0768 64666).

NEAREST RAILWAY STATION Penrith (10 miles).

The fells in autumn

LOCATION Lying within the Lakeland hills, the Haweswater valley is approached from the M6 at Shap (Junction 39) or Penrith (Junction 40) by taking the road to Bampton and following the sign to Haweswater or Mardale. A car park is situated at the southern end of the reservoir. NY/470108.

TENURE Management agreement over Naddle Forest (1222 acres) and wardening agreement over 22 000 acres from North West Water.

STATUS Partly SSSI. Within the Lake District National Park.

HIGHNAM WOODS, GLOUCESTERSHIRE

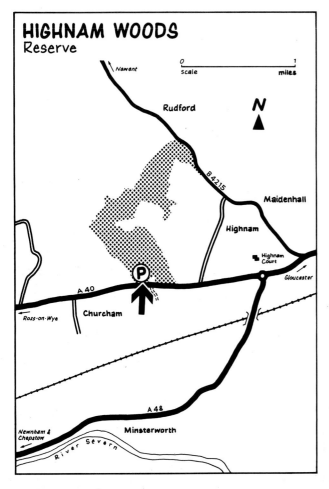

HIGHNAM WOODS
Reserve

Nawent
Rudford
B4215
Maidenhall
Highnam
Highnam Court
Gloucester
A40
Churcham
Ross-on-Wye
A48
Newnham & Chepstow
Minsterworth
River Severn

N

scale 0 miles 1

P

LOCATION Lying in the Severn Vale, 3½ miles west of Gloucester, this woodland is entered from the A40 Gloucester to Ross-on-Wye Road at SO/778190.

TENURE 294 acres owned.

WARDEN Peter Philp, The Coach House, Grove Farm, Taynton, near Gloucester GL19 3AM.

HABITAT Oak and ash woodland with some hazel and sweet chestnut coppice and an extensive network of rides.

BIRDS The resident birds include sparrowhawk, tawny owl, nuthatch, treecreeper, the three species of woodpecker and both marsh and willow tits, joined in summer by chiffchaff, blackcap, garden warbler, spotted flycatcher and a notable population of nightingales. Whitethroat, lesser whitethroat and grasshopper warbler breed in the scrub while moorhen and mallard nest on the ponds. Flocks of fieldfare and redwing, tits and finches occur in winter.

OTHER WILDLIFE Carpets of bluebells are enhanced by numerous cowslips and early purple orchids in spring. The rare Tintern (upright) spurge occurs plentifully in these woods whose ancient origin is indicated by wild service trees. Mammals include dormouse, fox and badger while purple hairstreak and white admiral are two of the butterflies.

VISITING Access at all times. Visitors are asked to keep to the waymarked paths.

FACILITIES   **P**

i St Michael's Tower, The Cross, Gloucester GL1 1PD (tel: 0452 421188).

NEAREST RAILWAY STATION Gloucester (3½ miles).

Treecreeper

HODBARROW, CUMBRIA

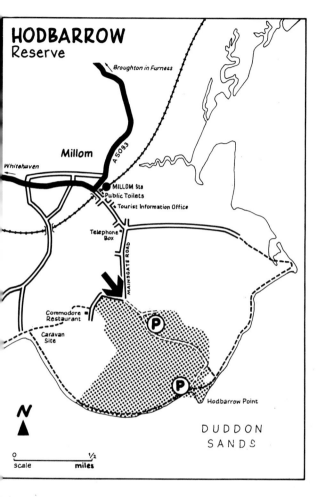

HODBARROW Reserve

BIRDS Little tern, oystercatcher and ringed plover nest on the sea bank. Many migrants including warblers frequent the scrub. Hundreds of wigeon, teal, mallard, goldeneye, red-breasted merganser and coot winter on the lagoon whose shores are used by oystercatcher, redshank and dunlin for roosting during high winter tides. There is a herd of over 50 mute swans.

OTHER WILDLIFE The rare natterjack toad breeds in shallow pools. Bloody cranesbill and several orchid species flower in the grassland.

VISITING Access at all times from the informal car parks along a footpath around the lagoon including the exposed sea-wall, with views also over the estuary.

FACILITIES P

i Millom Folk Museum, St George's Road, Millom LA18 4AF (tel: 0657 255).

NEAREST RAILWAY STATION Millom (2 miles).

Mute swan

LOCATION Lying beside the Duddon estuary, Hodbarrow is approached from Millom via Mainsgate Road, turning left at its end for the reserve entrance. SD/174791.

TENURE 260 acres owned.

STATUS SSSI.

WARDEN Doug Radford, 29 Mainsgate Road, Millom, Cumbria LA18 4JZ.

HABITAT Slightly brackish lagoon bordered by limestone scrub and grassland and the estuary bank.

HORNSEA MERE, HUMBERSIDE

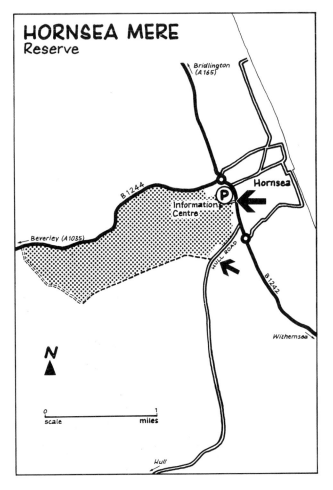

BIRDS Hundreds of reed warblers nest here as well as sedge warbler, reed bunting, coot and great crested grebe. Cormorants roost in the lakeside trees. Little gulls and black terns are often numerous on summer passage and wheatear, whinchat and various warblers pass during the spring. Winter brings large concentrations of goldeneye, mallard, coot, wigeon, teal, pochard and tufted duck to the mere.

OTHER WILDLIFE The mere is notable for its pike, perch and roach. Aquatic insects such as the great red sedge fly are plentiful.

VISITING Cars may be parked by the information centre on Kirkholme Point (by kind permission of Hornsea Mere Marine Company) where a cafeteria and boating are also available. Kirkholme Point is not part of the RSPB reserve, *therefore visitors are asked not to park their cars and leave the Point as the entrance gates may be locked at any time.* A public footpath along the south side of the mere, starting in Hull Road, provides good birdwatching. No other access is permitted to the reserve.

FACILITIES   P   WC   IC   G 30p

i   Floral Hall, Esplanade, Hornsea, Humberside (tel: 040 12 2919).

NEAREST RAILWAY STATION Beverley (12 miles).

The lake fringed by fen

LOCATION The reserve information centre is situated at the east end of the mere and is reached from the centre of Hornsea by taking the side roads signposted to The Mere. TA/202474.

TENURE 580 acres leased from the Wassand Estate.

STATUS SSSI. Grade 1. Also a Statutory Bird Sanctuary.

WARDEN Trevor Charlton, 11 Carlton Avenue, Hornsea, North Humberside HU18 1JG.

HABITAT A large natural, freshwater lake, reed-fringed and bordered by mixed woodland and farmland close to the sea.

LANGSTONE HARBOUR, HAMPSHIRE

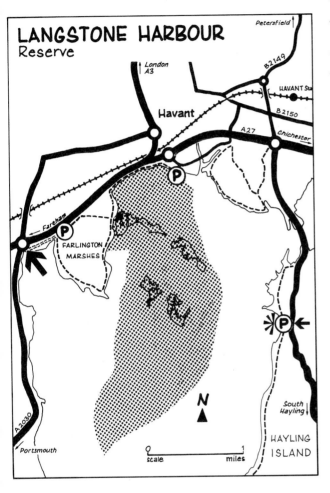

LANGSTONE HARBOUR
Reserve

LOCATION Occupying a central portion of Langstone Harbour, the reserve's low islands and mudflats may be viewed from the coastal footpath along the northern shore, also from the sea-wall of Farlington Marshes (a reserve of the Hampshire and Isle of Wight Naturalists' Trust).

TENURE 1370 acres owned.

STATUS SSSI. Grade 1*. SPA. Ramsar.

WARDEN Chris Tyas, c/o RSPB, South-East England Office (page 8).

HABITAT Mudflats and creeks with saltmarsh and shingle islands.

BIRDS The islands are the site of one of Britain's largest little tern colonies which numbered over 160 pairs in 1988. Common tern, ringed plover and redshank also breed there. The entire harbour is outstanding for wintering wildfowl including over 7000 brent geese as well as teal, wigeon, shelduck, dunlin, oystercatcher, curlew and black-tailed godwit. Black-necked grebe, red-breasted merganser and greenshank occur regularly outside the breeding season.

OTHER WILDLIFE Foxes sometimes visit the islands.

VISITING There is no official reserve entrance but good views may be obtained from the car park close to the roundabout at the junction of the A3 and A27 (SU/698057) and at the car park off the Hayling Island road by the Esso garage (SU/718029). Access to Farlington Marshes and good viewpoints may be gained from the roundabout at the junction of the A2030 and A27 Chichester to Fareham road (SU/675043). The reserve islands are subject to a restricted landing policy: the southern end of Long Island is open at all times and Round Nap outside the breeding season, all other areas being closed.
NB. Groups wishing to visit Farlington Marshes should book, well in advance, with the Hampshire and Isle of Wight Naturalists' Trust warden, 61 Southampton Road, Fareham, Hampshire PO16 7DZ (tel: 0329 280023).

_i_ The Hard, Portsmouth, Hampshire (tel: 0705 826722/3).

NEAREST RAILWAY STATION Havant (adjacent).

LEIGHTON MOSS, LANCASHIRE

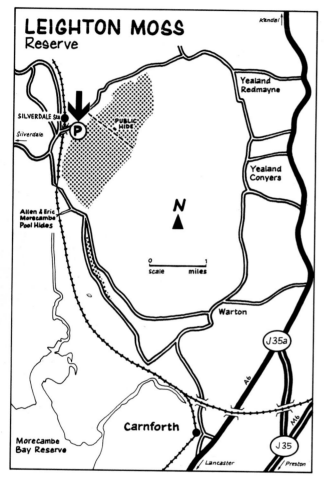

LOCATION Lying in a limestone valley close to the shore of Morecambe Bay, the reserve is entered close to Silverdale station and is reached from the A6(T) through Carnforth, Yealand Conyers or Yealand Redmayne. SD/478751.

TENURE 321 acres owned.

STATUS SSSI. Grade 1. SPA. Ramsar.

WARDEN John Wilson, Myers Farm, Silverdale, Carnforth LA5 0SW (tel: 0524 701601).

HABITAT A large reedswamp with meres and willow and alder scrub in a valley, with woodland on its limestone slopes.

BIRDS Britain's largest concentration of up to ten pairs of bitterns breed here, together with bearded tit, reed, sedge and grasshopper warblers, teal, shoveler, pochard, tufted duck and occasionally marsh harrier. Black tern and osprey regularly pass through in spring and greenshank and various sandpipers in autumn. Wintering wildfowl include large flocks of mallard, teal, wigeon, pintail and shoveler. Thousands of starlings, swallows and wagtails roost seasonally in the reeds, often attracting hunting sparrowhawks.

OTHER WILDLIFE Otters are resident and are frequently seen from the hides, as are roe and red deer.

VISITING Open on all days *except Tuesday*, 9.00am to 9.00pm or sunset when earlier. £2.00 charge for non-members. Five hides overlooking various meres are linked by paths through the reeds. One is on the public causeway and is open, free of charge, at all times. The reserve Centre contains interpretative displays, an exhibition and toilets. RSPB Birdshop open April to December daily 10.00am to 5.00pm; January to March weekends and Wednesdays only.

FACILITIES

Marine Road Central, Morecambe, Lancashire (tel: 0524 414110).

NEAREST RAILWAY STATION Silverdale (¼ mile).

Aerial view of the pools surrounded by reedbeds

THE LODGE, BEDFORDSHIRE

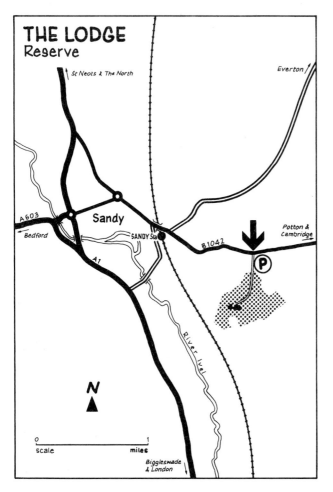

LOCATION The headquarters of the RSPB and its surrounding reserve is entered from the B1042 road to Cambridge, a mile east of Sandy which is on the A1. TL/192486.

TENURE 104 acres owned.

STATUS Partly SSSI.

WARDEN Mel Kemp, The Lodge, Sandy SG19 2DL (tel: 0767 80551).

HABITAT Mature woodland, pine plantations, birch and bracken slopes on a ridge of Lower Greensand with a remnant of heath and an artificial lake. Formal gardens adjoin the Victorian mansion.

BIRDS Breeding birds include kestrel, green and great spotted woodpeckers, nuthatch, treecreeper, blackcap, garden warbler, moorhen and tree pipit. Kingfisher, heron, sparrowhawk and crossbill are occasionally seen. Finches including siskin and redpoll occur in winter.

OTHER WILDLIFE Muntjac deer are often seen. Several species of dragonflies frequent the lake in summer. There is an important breeding colony of natterjack toads.

VISITING The reserve and formal gardens are open on all day from 9.00am to 9.00pm or sunset when earlier. The shop and reception with its exhibition is open all year 9.00am to 5.00pm weekdays; 10.00am to 5.00pm weekends (except for Christmas to Easter which is 12.00pm to 4.30pm). The house and other premises, being administrative offices, are *not* open to members or the public. There are four nature trails of various lengths (with leaflet) around the reserve and a hide overlooks the lake. £1.50 charge for non-members.

FACILITIES **P WC IC S** & **G** 40p

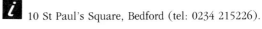

i 10 St Paul's Square, Bedford (tel: 0234 215226).

NEAREST RAILWAY STATION Sandy (1½ miles).

The woodlands in spring

LODMOOR, DORSET

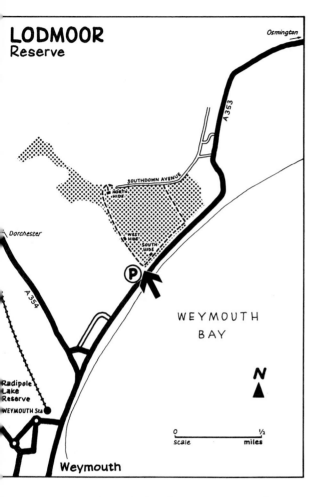

LODMOOR
Reserve

BIRDS The reedbeds and scrub contain reed, sedge and grasshopper warblers, bearded tit, reed bunting and Cetti's warbler, while mallard, redshank and yellow wagtail breed on the marsh. Thousands of yellow wagtails congregate on migration and a variety of waders such as greenshank and green sandpiper use the pools to feed and rest. Wintering wildfowl include mallard, teal, shoveler, wigeon, shelduck and brent geese.

OTHER WILDLIFE The large black and yellow spider *Argiope bruennichi* frequents the grassy banks.

VISITING Access at all times from the public car park to a perimeter path which links three hides overlooking the marsh and reedbeds. See under Radipole Lake for the Weymouth car parking concession (page 60).

FACILITIES P WC &

i Pavilion Theatre Complex, The Esplanade, Weymouth, Dorset (tel: 0305 772444).

NEAREST RAILWAY STATION Weymouth (1½ miles).

Yellow wagtail

LOCATION Situated near the beach on the east side of Weymouth, the reserve is entered from the Preston Road car park on the A353 road to Wareham as signposted. SY/687807.

TENURE 150 acres leased from Weymouth Borough Council.

STATUS SSSI.

WARDEN Doug Ireland, c/o Radipole Lake Reserve (see page 60).

HABITAT A marsh with shallow pools, reeds and scrub as well as remnant saltmarsh inside the seawall.

49

MINSMERE, SUFFOLK

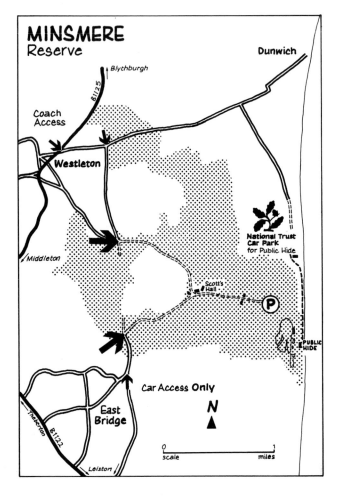

HABITAT The famous Scrape – an area of shallow brackish water, mud and islands inside the shingle beach – as well as extensive reedbeds with meres and both heathland and deciduous woodland.

BIRDS A large variety of breeding birds include common tern and Britain's second largest avocet colony on the Scrape; little tern on the beach; bittern, marsh harrier, bearded tit and water rail in the reeds; nightjar and stonechat on the heath and nightingale and redstart in the woods. Many different waders such as spotted redshank, black-tailed godwit, little stint and several rarities use the Scrape on migration. Bewick's swan, wigeon, gadwall and teal occur in winter.

OTHER WILDLIFE Water voles and otters frequent the marshes, red deer and muntjac the woods, while adders and silver-studded blue butterflies are encountered on the heath.

VISITING Open on all days *except Tuesday*, 9.00am to 9.00pm or sunset when earlier. £2.00 charge for non-members. Car drivers are asked to take special care on the narrow lanes within and approaching the reserve. The public hide on the beach overlooking the Scrape is always open (free of charge) and is reached on foot from Dunwich Cliffs National Trust car park (TM/475680).

FACILITIES P WC IC S & G 50p

ℹ Town Hall, High Street, Southwold, Suffolk (tel: 0502 722366).

NEAREST RAILWAY STATION Saxmundham (6 miles).

Freshwater marshland

LOCATION Lying on the low Suffolk coast, this premier RSPB reserve is reached either from Westleton or through East Bridge (*no coaches this way*) from the B1122 road from Leiston to Yoxford. It is clearly signposted in the vicinity. TM/452680.

TENURE 1470 acres owned.

STATUS SSSI. Grade 1*. Ramsar. Council of Europe Diploma.

WARDEN Jeremy Sorensen, Minsmere Reserve, Westleton, Saxmundham IP17 2BY (tel: 072 873 281).

MORECAMBE BAY, LANCASHIRE

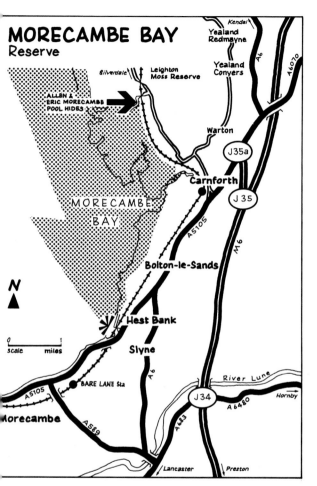

MORECAMBE BAY
Reserve

N

WARDEN John Wilson, c/o Leighton Moss Reserve (see page 46).

HABITAT Extensive sheep-grazed saltmarsh and inter-tidal sandflats with some artificial brackish water pools on the inner side.

BIRDS Of outstanding importance for its very large flocks of waders such as knot, dunlin, oystercatcher, curlew, bar-tailed godwit and redshank which congregate, according to the tides, during most of the year except mid-summer. Sanderling occur on May migration. Peregrines frequently hunt the waders in winter when shelduck, pintail, wigeon, red-breasted merganser and greylag are present. Oystercatcher, redshank and wheatear nest on the saltings.

OTHER WILDLIFE Bloody cranesbill, rock-rose and rock samphire flower on the limestone cliffs behind the marsh at Silverdale.

VISITING Access to Hest Bank and the Carnforth Marsh pool hides at all times. Tide times are available from Leighton Moss Reserve. *Visitors are warned to beware of dangerous channels and quicksands on the foreshore.*

FACILITIES **P** ♿ (Hest Bank)

ℹ️ Marine Road Central, Morecambe, Lancashire (tel: 0524 414110).

NEAREST RAILWAY STATION Silverdale (1 mile to Carnforth Marsh) and Bare Lane (2 miles to Hest Bank).

Aerial view of the bay

LOCATION The eastern side of this vast estuary may be viewed from several vantage points, notably the car park across the level-crossing at Hest Bank off the A5105 Morecambe to Carnforth road (SD/468666). A small car park off the Carnforth to Silverdale road near Leighton Moss Reserve (see page 46) provides access to hides overlooking large pools on the Carnforth saltings (SD/476737).

TENURE 3750 acres owned, together with a further 2400 acres of freehold rights.

STATUS SSSI. Grade 1*.

NAGSHEAD, GLOUCESTERSHIRE

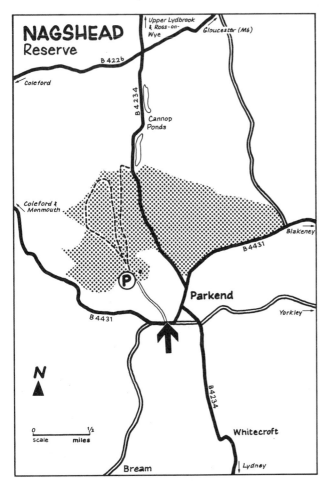

LOCATION Forming part of the ancient Forest of Dean, this reserve is situated immediately west of Parkend village and is signposted off the B4431 road to Coleford. SO/612078.

TENURE 761 acres managed by agreement with the Forestry Commission.

STATUS SSSI. Grade 1.

WARDEN Ivan Proctor, 15 Forest Road, Milkwall, Coleford GL16 7LB.

HABITAT Mature oakwood with beech, birch, rowan and holly and containing a rocky stream with a pool and clumps of alder and firs.

BIRDS A large population of pied flycatchers nest mainly in boxes, as do some of the redstarts, great and blue tits and nuthatches. Other breeding species include wood warbler, chiffchaff, tree pipit, blackcap, garden warbler, treecreeper and the three species of woodpeckers. Sparrowhawk, crossbill and hawfinch are seen regularly.

OTHER WILDLIFE Bluebells and foxgloves are abundant. Silver-washed and pearl-bordered fritillaries and white admiral butterflies occur, as do dormice and fallow deer.

VISITING Access at all times from the reserve car park and picnic area. Visitors are asked to keep to the waymarked paths of 1 mile and 2 miles in length. There are two hides overlooking glades and a pool. Information centre open at weekends mid-April to August.

FACILITIES **P IC G** 30p

i Cinderford Library, Bell View Road, Cinderford, Gloucestershire (tel: 0594 22581).

NEAREST RAILWAY STATION Lydney (6 miles).

Female redstart

NENE WASHES, CAMBRIDGESHIRE

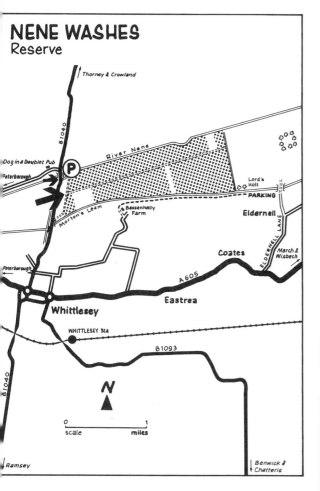

BIRDS Black-tailed godwit, lapwing, redshank, snipe, sedge warbler, yellow wagtail, shoveler, mallard, gadwall and shelduck nest regularly, with garganey in some years. Marsh harrier and hobby occur in summer while several waders such as greenshank pause on migration. When flooding occurs in winter large flocks of Bewick's swan, wigeon, teal, shoveler and pintail visit the reserve.

OTHER WILDLIFE Greater bladderwort, flowering rush and water violet flower in the ditches which attract several dragonfly species.

VISITING Until proper facilities have been installed, members and the public are welcome to visit the reserve *by written application to the warden*.

FACILITIES P

i Town Hall, Bridge Street, Peterborough, Cambridgeshire (tel: 0733 63141).

NEAREST RAILWAY STATION Whittlesey (2 miles).

Lapwing

LOCATION This Fenland reserve is situated five miles east of Peterborough and is entered off the B1040 road from Whittlesey to Thorney. TL/277992.

TENURE 665 acres owned.

STATUS SSSI. Grade 1.

WARDEN Geoff Welch, 21a East Delph, Whittlesey, near Peterborough PE7 1RH.

HABITAT A three-mile stretch of wet meadows with a bunded area of marshland between two embanked rivers.

NOR MARSH AND MOTNEY HILL, KENT

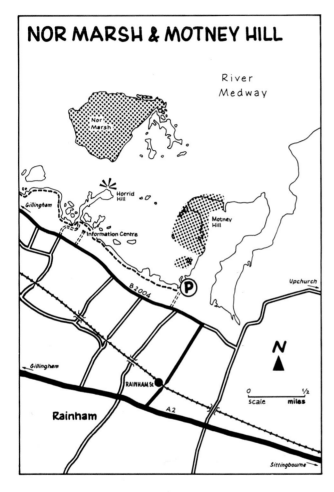

LOCATION Forming part of the Medway estuary, these two areas lie east of Gillingham and are reached via the B2004 Lower Rainham Road out of Chatham.

TENURE 251 acres leased from Gillingham Borough Council.

STATUS SSSI. Grade 1.

WARDEN Alan Parker, Swigshole Cottage, High Halstow, Rochester ME3 8SR.

HABITAT Saltmarsh and intertidal mud.

BIRDS Common terns nest on the island of Nor Marsh where little and Sandwich terns occur in autumn. The saltings and tidal water off Motney Hill attract numerous great crested and some rarer grebes in winter together with brent geese, goldeneye, red-breasted merganser and pintail. Waders are abundant including many black-tailed godwits in spring and autumn and passage whimbrel in July.

OTHER WILDLIFE Essex skipper, short-winged conehead and Roesel's bush cricket are some of the more interesting insects.

VISITING Nor Marsh can be viewed from the end of Horrid Hill (TQ/811689), with parking in the Riverside Country Park. *Visitors must not walk out over the old causeway to the island.* Access at all times to the sea-wall and edge of the bay by Motney Hill by driving down Motney Hill Road and using the small car park on the left (TQ/825680) – but *not* further along the private road please.

i Eastgate Cottage, High Street, Rochester ME1 1EW (tel: 0634 43666).

NEAREST RAILWAY STATION Gillingham (3 miles) or Rainham (2 miles).

Goldeneye drake

NORTHWARD HILL, KENT

NORTHWARD HILL
Reserve

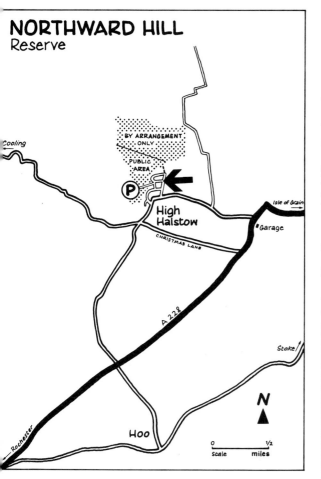

LOCATION Overlooking the Thames marshes north of Rochester, the reserve lies on rising ground at the edge of High Halstow which is reached via the A228 road to the Isle of Grain. Then follow the brown road signs. The reserve is entered across a field from Northwood Avenue in High Halstow – follow the brown road signs. TQ/784759.

TENURE 134 acres owned.

STATUS SSSI. Grade 2. Also a National Nature Reserve.

WARDEN Alan Parker, Swigshole Cottage, High Halstow, Rochester ME3 8SR.

HABITAT Deciduous woodland of oak, ash and maple with elm scrub and dense thickets of hawthorn.

BIRDS The location of Britain's largest heronry of some 220 pairs which feed on the marshes below. Many nightingale and turtle dove breed as well as whitethroat, lesser whitethroat, garden warbler, blackcap and both great and lesser spotted woodpeckers. Merlin and sparrowhawk frequently prey on the thrush roosts in winter.

OTHER WILDLIFE A thriving colony of white-letter hairstreak butterflies occupies the elm scrub. Essex skipper and speckled wood also occur.

VISITING The paths in the public part of the reserve are accessible at all times. Escorted access to the sanctuary area, including the heronry viewpoint, may be arranged by written application to the warden (charge £1 to non-members), the herons being present from February to July. Please note that coaches are not advisable owing to the difficulties of parking in High Halstow.

i Eastgate Cottage, High Street, Rochester, Kent (tel: 0634 43666).

NEAREST RAILWAY STATION Rochester (6 miles).

Heronry

NORTH WARREN, SUFFOLK

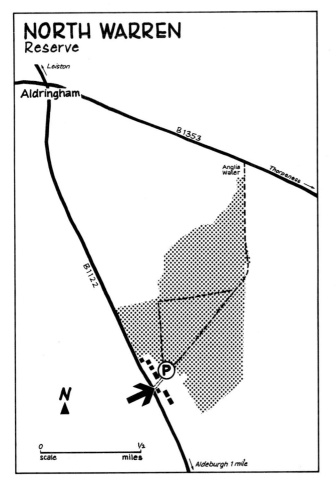

NORTH WARREN
Reserve

Leiston
Aldringham
B1353
Thorpeness
Anglia water
B1122
P
N▲
0   ½
scale   miles
Aldeburgh 1 mile

HABITAT A grass heath with areas of gorse and birch scrub on sandy soil, together with a mature fen with reeds, meadowsweet and sallow.

BIRDS Yellowhammer, skylark, linnet, whitethroat and nightingale nest on the scrubby heath where wheatears occur on migration. Reed, sedge and grasshopper warblers and reed bunting frequent the fen and both kingfisher and bearded tit are seen occasionally.

OTHER WILDLIFE Viper's bugloss, mullein and tree lupin flower on the heath.

VISITING Access at all times to a nature trail which explores the reserve.

FACILITIES **P**

i The Cinema, High Street, Aldeburgh, Suffolk (tel: 072 885 3637).

NEAREST RAILWAY STATION Saxmundham (6 miles).

Reed warbler feeding young

LOCATION Part of the Sandlings heathland of the Suffolk coast, this reserve lies on the east side of the B1122 road to Leiston a mile north of Aldeburgh. The car park is entered, as signposted, between the neighbouring houses. TM/455587.

TENURE 237 acres owned.

STATUS SSSI.

WARDEN None present. Enquiries to Minsmere Reserve (see page 50).

OLD HALL MARSHES, ESSEX

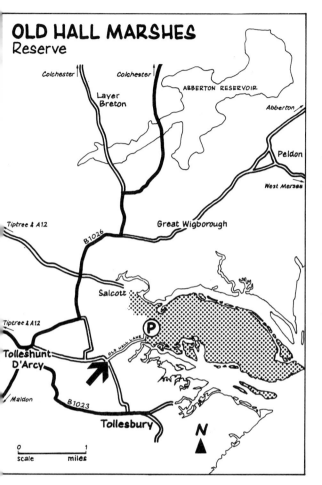

OLD HALL MARSHES Reserve

LOCATION This remote peninsula at the mouth of the Blackwater estuary is entered at its western end from the minor road between Tollesbury and Tolleshunt D'Arcy. TL/950117.

TENURE 1118 acres owned and 442 acres leased from the Nature Conservancy Council.

STATUS SSSI. Grade 1*.

WARDEN Malcolm Stott, 5 Old Hall Lane, Tolleshunt D'Arcy, Maldon, Essex.

HABITAT Extensive grazing marshes with freshwater fleets and reedbeds, saltings and two small offshore islands.

BIRDS Up to 4000 brent geese feed on the improved pasture each winter when thousands of wigeon, teal, shelduck, grey plover, curlew, redshank and dunlin frequent the marshes. Divers and goldeneye are seen on the adjacent channels and short-eared owl, hen harrier, barn owl and merlin regularly hunt the reserve. Breeding species include redshank, pochard, shoveler, bearded tit, water rail and common tern. Waders such as avocet visit on migration.

OTHER WILDLIFE Yellow ants form their mounds in the ancient grassland. The scarce emerald damselfly has been recorded.

VISITING *Entry by written permit only from the warden* on all days *except Tuesdays* from 9.00am to 9.00pm or sunset when earlier. Car drivers are asked *to take special care* on the narrow approach lane with its 20mph speed restriction.

FACILITIES P

i 2 High Street, Maldon, Essex (tel: 0621 56503).

NEAREST RAILWAY STATION Kelvedon (9 miles).

Saltmarsh in the Blackwater estuary

OUSE WASHES, CAMBRIDGESHIRE

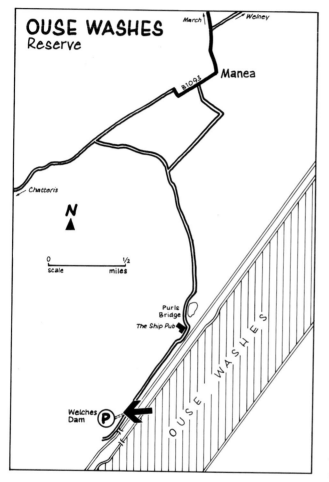

LOCATION Part of a 19-mile stretch of flood washland, the RSPB reserve is entered at Welches Dam which is signposted from Manea village. Approach via the B1093 or B1098 roads from the A141 road from Chatteris to March. TL/471861. (*NB:* the area hatched is not entirely owned by the RSPB.)

TENURE 1856 acres owned.

STATUS SSSI. Grade 1*. Ramsar.

WARDEN Cliff Carson, Limosa, Welches Dam, Manea, March PE15 0NF.

HABITAT Extensive wet meadowland or 'washes', dissected by numerous ditches and contained by two parallel rivers that were excavated in the 17th century. Several osier beds grow by the River Delph.

BIRDS The largest concentration of black-tailed godwits in Britain (about 20 pairs) breed on this and the adjacent Wildfowl Trust and Cambridgeshire Wildlife Trust reserves, their success depending on the state of flooding in the spring. Ruffs 'lek' annually and may nest; other breeding species include shoveler, teal, garganey, yellow wagtail, lapwing, redshank and snipe. In winter, when the washes are flooded, this becomes the most important site inland in Britain for wildfowl including some 5000 Bewick's swans and huge numbers of wigeon, teal, pintail and mallard as well as shoveler, whooper swan, hen harrier and merlin.

OTHER WILDLIFE A rich variety of aquatic plants includes fringed water-lily, flowering rush, brooklime and arrowhead.

VISITING Access at all times from the reserve car park, with Information Centre (open weekends and Bank holidays) and toilets, to a series of hides (provided by both the Society and CWT) overlooking the washes. Visitors are requested to walk below and behind the bank to avoid disturbing the birds. Sundays are preferable to Saturdays during September–January when wildfowling on adjacent non-reserve washes may cause disturbance. Details of special escorted walks and boat trips from the warden.

FACILITIES P WC IC G 30p

i Public Library, Palace Green, Ely, Cambridgeshire (tel: 0353 2062).

NEAREST RAILWAY STATION Manea (3 miles).

PILSEY ISLAND, WEST SUSSEX

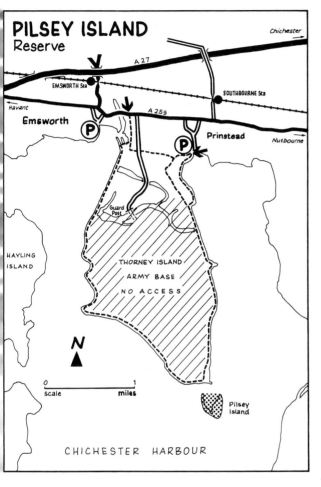

BIRDS The site of the largest wader roost in Chichester Harbour, notably of oystercatcher, grey plover, sanderling, dunlin and bar-tailed godwit. In winter up to 1500 brent geese may be seen with smaller numbers of duck. Ringed plover, redshank and shelduck nest here.

OTHER WILDLIFE The plants include sea spurge and yellow-horned poppy.

VISITING No visiting permitted but excellent views of the island and wader roosts can be obtained from Longmere Point (SU/768010) on the coastal footpath around Thorney Island. This path, a seven-mile circuit, can be reached from Emsworth (car park at SU/749056) or Prinsted (car park at SU/766051). *NB:* Strictly no access to Thorney Island Army Base.

ℹ️ St Peter's Market, West Street, Chichester PO19 1AH (tel: 0243 775888).

NEAREST RAILWAY STATION Emsworth (1½ miles).

Grey plover

LOCATION This small island lies off the southern tip of Thorney Island in the centre of Chichester Harbour.

TENURE 45 acres leased from the Ministry of Defence.

STATUS SSSI. Grade 1*. SPA. Ramsar.

WARDEN Chris Tyas, c/o South-East England Office (page 8), usually assisted by a seasonal warden from April to July.

HABITAT Shingle, sand dunes and saltmarsh.

RADIPOLE LAKE, DORSET

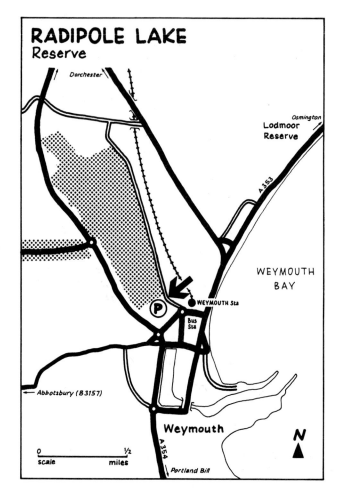

RADIPOLE LAKE
Reserve

LOCATION Situated within the town of Weymouth, the reserve information centre and entrance are located beside the Swannery public car park which is signposted from the main street along the seafront. SY/677796.

TENURE 192 acres leased from Weymouth Borough Council.

STATUS SSSI. Also Statutory Bird Sanctuary.

WARDEN Doug Ireland, 52 Goldcroft Avenue, Weymouth DT4 0ES.

HABITAT Large reedbeds and lakes with rough pasture, scrub and some artificial shallow lagoons.

BIRDS Reed, sedge and grasshopper warblers, bearded tit, great crested grebe, mute swan, kingfisher and many Cetti's warblers breed here, while heron, cormorant, shelduck and sparrowhawk visit regularly. Up to 100 mute swans congregate to moult, while considerable numbers of yellow wagtails, sedge warblers and swallows roost in the reeds during migration. Mediterranean and other uncommon species of gulls occur. Shoveler, teal and pochard are among the wintering duck.

OTHER WILDLIFE Interesting dragonflies include the emperor.

VISITING Access to the reserve at all times. The Centre (with its panoramic window overlooking the lake) is open daily throughout the year except for October–March (weekends only). Public toilets are available in the adjacent car park (for which there is a charge). A ticket purchased *first* in the Swannery car park allows parking without charge in that for Lodmoor (page 49). Firm paths lead to three hides, two of which are for members and permit holders only. The facilities have all been designed with the needs of handicapped visitors in mind, including 'listening posts' and a tap-rail on the trail, and audio-loop in the centre.

FACILITIES P WC IC & G 50p

i Pavilion Theatre Complex, The Esplanade, Weymouth, Dorset (tel: 0305 772444).

NEAREST RAILWAY STATION Weymouth (adjacent).

RYE HOUSE MARSH, HERTFORDSHIRE

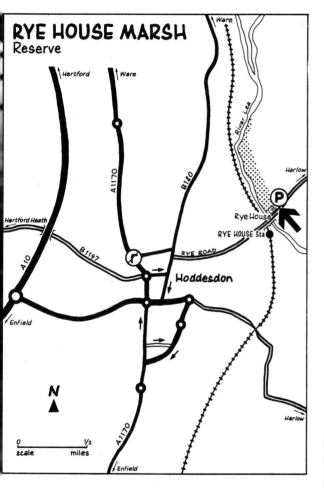

RYE HOUSE MARSH
Reserve

Hertford
Ware
Ware
A1170
B180
River Lea
Harlow
Hertford Heath
B1197
P
Rye House
RYE HOUSE Sta
RYE ROAD
A10
Enfield
Hoddesdon
N
Harlow
A1170
Enfield

0   ½
scale   miles

LOCATION Lying within the Lee Valley Regional Park, this reserve is approached from the A10 to Hoddesdon and, taking Rye Road, entering the car park just past Rye House railway station. TL/387099.

TENURE 13 acres leased from the Lee Valley Regional Park Authority.

WARDEN Kevin Roberts, Toad Cottage, 4 Cecil Road, Rye Park, Hoddesdon EN11 0JA.

HABITAT A riverside marsh containing a variety of habitats including flood meadows, shallow pools and mud, fen, stands of reed and reed sweet-grass, willow and alder scrub and wet woodland.

BIRDS Mallard, tufted duck, coot, moorhen, cuckoo, reed and sedge warblers breed regularly and common terns nest on rafts on the adjacent lakes. Green and common sandpipers, many hirundines, warblers and yellow wagtails occur on migration. Many snipe and teal are present in winter when kingfisher, water rail, jack snipe, siskin and occasionally bittern and bearded tit may be seen. Meadow pipits, yellowhammers and corn buntings roost on the marsh in winter.

OTHER WILDLIFE Pink water speedwell, fen bedstraw and ragged robin are among the plants. Water vole, harvest mouse and grass snake are present.

VISITING Although this is primarily an educational reserve for schoolchildren, members and the public are welcome to visit it at weekends. £1 charge for non-members. Access is also made available on weekdays whenever possible. The South Hide is always open but for access to the rest of the reserve and other hides, please telephone Hoddesdon (0992) 460031. The South Hide is accessible to wheelchairs along a short concrete path. Educational staff are available to receive schoolchildren of all ages as well as groups in further and higher education, by appointment, for field studies.

FACILITIES **P WC IC** &

i Vale House, 43 Cowbridge, Hertford (tel: 0279 55261).

NEAREST RAILWAY STATION Rye House (300 yards).

Cuckoo

ST BEES HEAD, CUMBRIA

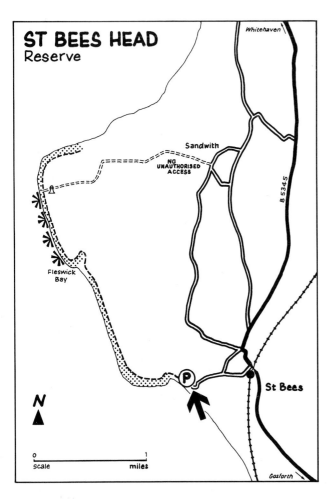

ST BEES HEAD Reserve

Whitehaven

Sandwith

NO UNAUTHORISED ACCESS

B5345

Fleswick Bay

St Bees

Gosforth

N

0 scale 1 miles

BIRDS One of the largest cliff seabird colonies on the west coast of England containing razorbill, guillemot, kittiwake, herring gull, fulmar, a small number of puffins and the only black guillemots breeding in England. Rock pipit, raven, peregrine, stonechat, whitethroat, shag and cormorant also frequent the cliffs. Gannet, skuas, terns, shearwaters and eider may be seen offshore at various times.

OTHER WILDLIFE Rock samphire, bloody cranesbill and heath spotted orchid flower on the cliff-top.

VISITING A public footpath from the public car park (NX/962118) on St Bees beach goes north along the cliffs to four safe observation points. Only cars with disabled visitors may use the private road to the lighthouse from Sandwith – otherwise *no access*. Visitors should not attempt to reach the beach between the north and south headlands other than at Fleswick Bay.

FACILITIES P WC &

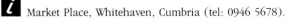 Market Place, Whitehaven, Cumbria (tel: 0946 5678).

NEAREST RAILWAY STATION St Bees (½ mile).

Razorbills and guillemots

LOCATION This cliff headland lies south of Whitehaven and west of the B5345 road to St Bees. NX/962118.

TENURE 3 miles of cliffs, in two parts, owned.

STATUS SSSI.

WARDEN Present from April to August, c/o Sandwith Post Office, near Whitehaven, Cumbria.

HABITAT Sandstone cliffs, up to 300ft high, with many ledges and grassy tops with gorse patches.

SANDWELL VALLEY, BIRMINGHAM

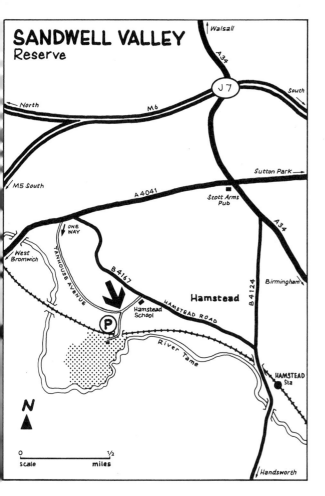

LOCATION Forming part of the Sandwell Valley Country Park only four miles from the centre of Birmingham, the reserve is entered off Tanhouse Avenue which is reached via Hamstead Road in Great Barr. SP/036931.

TENURE 25 acres leased from Sandwell Valley Borough Council.

WARDEN Tony Whitehead, RSPB Nature Centre, 20 Tanhouse Avenue, Great Barr B43 5AG (tel: 021 358 3013).

HABITAT Part of a lake with an island, bordered by a marsh with willows, reed sweet-grass and shallow pools.

BIRDS Breeding birds include mallard, tufted duck, coot, moorhen, little ringed plover, lapwing, snipe, reed, sedge and willow warblers, whitethroat and willow tit. Common tern and great crested grebe occur in the summer. Curlew, dunlin, green and common sandpipers and greenshank visit on migration. Wigeon and pochard frequent the lake in winter, with teal in the marsh where snipe, jack snipe and water rail may be seen daily.

OTHER WILDLIFE Many species of butterflies are seen each year. Chicory and coltsfoot flower on the higher ground.

VISITING Access at all times to the car park from where firm paths lead to four hides overlooking the marsh, lake and wader scrape. The Information Centre, with shop and toilets, provides a panoramic view of the reserve. School parties from primary to sixth-form level are welcome by appointment. £1 charge for non-members.

FACILITIES P WC IC S & G 50p

i The Piazza National Exhibition Centre, Birmingham (tel: 021 780 4141).

NEAREST RAILWAY STATION Hamstead (1 mile).

Snipe

SNETTISHAM, NORFOLK

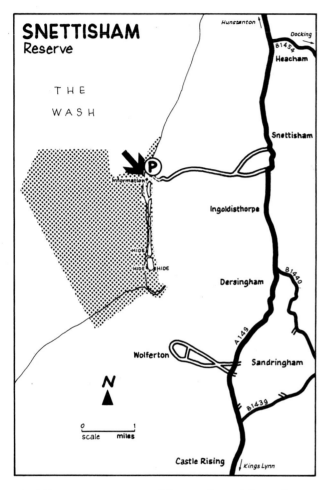

SNETTISHAM
Reserve

THE WASH

Hunstanton

Docking

B1454

Heacham

Snettisham

Ingoldisthorpe

HIDE
HIDE HIDE

Dersingham

B1440

Wolferton

A149

Sandringham

B1439

N

scale   miles
0   1

Castle Rising   Kings Lynn

Information
P

LOCATION Occupying part of the east shore of the Wash estuary, the beach and reserve are reached from Snettisham village on the A149 road from King's Lynn to Hunstanton. TF/648335.

TENURE 107 acres owned and 3150 acres leased from three owners.

STATUS SSSI. Grade 1*. SPA. Ramsar.

WARDEN 18 Cockle Road, Snettisham, near King's Lynn PE31 6HD.

HABITAT A shingle beach containing flooded pits borders a vast expanse of tidal sand and mudflats with saltmarsh.

BIRDS In winter up to 70 000 waders roost off the beach and on the artificial islands of the sanctuary pit during high tides. These include knot, grey plover, bar-tailed godwit, oystercatcher, dunlin, redshank, curlew, turnstone and ringed plover. Thousands of pink-footed and brent geese with shelduck, mallard, wigeon, pintail and teal use the foreshore for feeding and roosting. Diving ducks such as red-breasted merganser, tufted duck and scaup also frequent the pits which in summer have a nesting colony of common terns. Large numbers of sanderling and several passerines such as wheatear pause on migration.

OTHER WILDLIFE The shingle beach flora includes yellow-horned poppy, sea beet and hoary mullein.

VISITING Access at all times to the reserve beach and three hides to which visitors are required to walk (passing the holiday chalets) from the public car park. *Only cars with disabled visitors* may drive down and through the reserve gate at the southern end of the chalets.

FACILITIES   P   IC   &   G   30p

i The Green, Hunstanton, Norfolk (tel: 048 53 2610).

NEAREST RAILWAY STATION King's Lynn (12 miles).

Flooded shingle pits

STOUR WOOD AND COPPERAS BAY, ESSEX

STOUR WOOD & COPPERAS BAY
Reserve

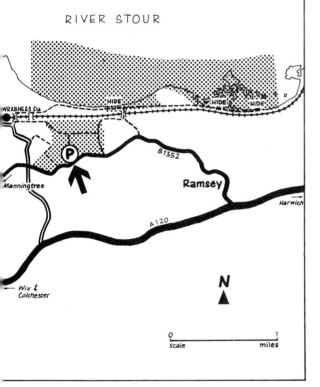

RIVER STOUR

WARDEN Russell Leavett, 24 Orchard Close, Great Oakley, Harwich CO12 5AX.

HABITAT The woodland is predominantly of oak and sweet chestnut with extensive chestnut coppice that is cut rotationally. Copperas Bay contains mudflats fringed by a little saltmarsh, reedbed and scrubby fields.

BIRDS Nightingale, garden warbler, blackcap, lesser whitethroat and both great and lesser spotted woodpeckers inhabit the woods and scrub. A variety of waterfowl feed in the bay in autumn and winter including wigeon, teal, pintail, shelduck, brent geese, redshank, curlew, grey plover and a notably large flock of black-tailed godwits.

OTHER WILDLIFE Butcher's broom, yellow archangel and wild service tree occur in Stour Wood with dormice and a colony of white admiral butterflies.

VISITING Access at all times along waymarked paths which lead from the car park through Stour Wood to three hides overlooking the bay – a round trip of four miles.

FACILITIES P

i Parkeston Quay, Harwich, Essex (tel: 0255 506139).

NEAREST RAILWAY STATION Wrabness (1 mile).

Saltmarsh on Copperas Bay

LOCATION Including most of Copperas Bay in the south-east of the Stour estuary west of Harwich, the reserve is entered in Stour Wood off the B1352 road from Manningtree to Ramsey one mile east of Wrabness Village. TM/189309.

TENURE Stour Wood (134 acres) is leased from the Woodland Trust. Most of Copperas Bay and the north part of Copperas Wood are owned (583 acres) with 70 acres of foreshore also leased from the Crown.

STATUS SSSI. Grade 1.

STRUMPSHAW FEN, NORFOLK

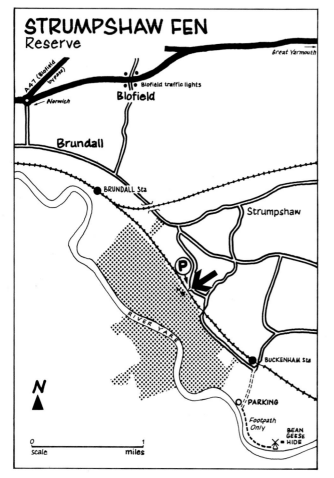

LOCATION Situated in the Yare Valley in the southern part of the Broads, the reserve is reached from the A47 Norwich to Yarmouth road by turning through Brundall. Beyond the railway bridge turn sharp right and right again into Low Road which leads to the reserve car park. To reach the reception hide, visitors must cross the level-crossing on foot *with care*. TG/342066.

TENURE 128 acres owned and 319 acres leased from W S Key.

STATUS SSSI. Grade 1*.

WARDEN Mike Blackburn, Staithe Cottage, Low Road, Strumpshaw, Norwich NR13 4HS.

HABITAT A large fen with reed and sedge beds, alder and willow stands, damp woodland and two broads beside the River Yare; also wet grazing marshes.

BIRDS Marsh harrier, bearded tit, Cetti's warbler, kingfisher, pochard, water rail, great crested grebe, gadwall, tufted duck and reed warbler nest in the fen, with redshank, snipe and yellow wagtail in the marshes. Cuckoos are plentiful; woodcock, nuthatch, treecreeper and the three species of woodpecker frequent the woodland. Wigeon as well as the largest flock of bean geese in Britain occur in winter, notably on the adjacent Buckenham Marshes, where there is a roost of hen harriers in the fen.

OTHER WILDLIFE Swallowtail butterflies are seen especially in June. Chinese water deer, grass snake and 20 species of dragonflies are present. Marsh pea, purple loosestrife and marsh sow-thistle flower in the fen.

VISITING Open all days from 9.00am to 9.00pm or sunset when earlier. A waymarked path encircles the fen and includes two hides (one of which is elevated). Another hide with an information annex overlooks the main broad. Fen nature trails interpret the diverse wildlife from late June to August. From November to February a public hide is open at all times by the Buckenham Marshes from which to watch the bean geese and wigeon. Best late December to early February. It is reached over the level-crossing at Buckenham station (TG/354045). £1.50 charge for non-members.

FACILITIES **P** **WC** **IC** **G** 50p

i Augustine Stewart House, 14 Tombland, Norwich (tel: 0603 666071).

NEAREST RAILWAY STATION Buckenham (1 mile).

Kingfisher

SURLINGHAM CHURCH MARSH, NORFOLK

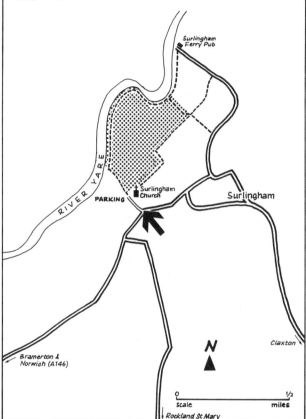

SURLINGHAM CHURCH MARSH
Reserve

LOCATION Lying on the south bank of the Yare river, the reserve is entered on foot from Surlingham church which is reached off the A146 road from Norwich to Lowestoft. TG/306064.

TENURE 68 acres owned.

STATUS SSSI. Grade 1*.

WARDEN Tony Baker, 2 Chapel Cottages, The Green, Surlingham, Norwich NR14 7AG.

HABITAT A former grazing marsh containing dykes and pools with reed, sedge, and some alder and willow scrub.

BIRDS Breeding birds include little grebe, mute swan, water rail, little ringed plover, common tern, shelduck, gadwall, teal, shoveler, pochard and tufted duck. Marsh harrier bred here in 1988. Reed, sedge and grasshopper warblers nest regularly while Cetti's and Savi's warblers occur in some years. Green and wood sandpipers and greenshank occur on passage and water pipit, hen harrier and jack snipe are among the winter visitors.

OTHER WILDLIFE Wetland plants include frogbit, bogbean, early and southern marsh orchids, marsh cinquefoil and marsh sow-thistle. Frogs, toads and grass snakes are common and dragonflies are numerous in late summer when the 'hawkers' are well represented.

VISITING Access at all times along the waymarked paths from which two hides overlook the marsh and pools. Visitors are asked to park *carefully* by the church where space is limited.

 Augustine Stewart House, 14 Tombland, Norwich (tel: 0603 666071).

NEAREST RAILWAY STATION Norwich (6 miles).

Little grebe

TETNEY MARSHES, LINCOLNSHIRE

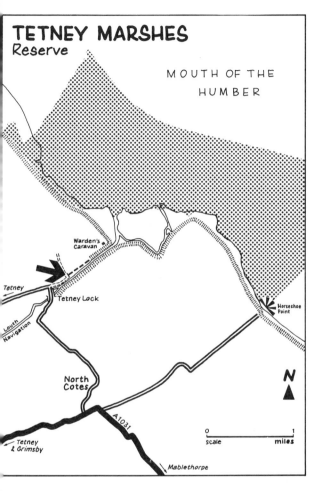

TETNEY MARSHES
Reserve

MOUTH OF THE HUMBER

Warden's Caravan

Tetney

Tetney Lock

Louth Navigation

Horseshoe Point

North Cotes

A1031

Tetney & Grimsby

Mablethorpe

N

0 scale 1 miles

LOCATION Lying near the mouth of the Humber estuary, the reserve may be entered *on foot* via the locked entrance gate or the riverbank east of Tetney lock. This is east of Tetney village which is on the A1031 south from Cleethorpes. TA/345025.

TENURE 436 acres leased with 2675 acres held by agreement from adjacent owners.

STATUS SSSI. Grade 1*.

WARDEN Present from April to August, c/o The Post Office, Tetney, Grimsby, South Humberside.

HABITAT Extensive sandflats bordered by low sand dunes and a wide saltmarsh with creeks.

BIRDS The site of one of Britain's largest colonies of little terns which nest at the tide's edge. Shelduck, oystercatcher, ringed plover and redshank also breed. Several migrant species, including whimbrel, occur and wigeon, teal, brent geese, oystercatcher, grey and golden plovers, bar-tailed godwit and knot flock in winter.

OTHER WILDLIFE Grey seals may be seen occasionally.

VISITING Access at all times. Good views are obtained from the sea-wall, especially at high tide. Visitors should avoid the saltmarsh and sand dunes because of the *dangerous tides*. The little tern colony must not be disturbed.

i 43 Alexandra Road, Cleethorpes, Humberside (tel: 0472 697472).

NEAREST RAILWAY STATION Cleethorpes (8 miles).

Teal drake

TITCHWELL MARSH, NORFOLK

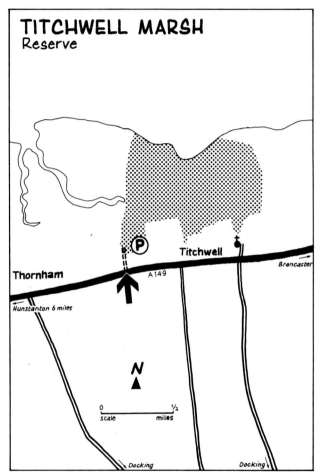

HABITAT Both tidal and freshwater reedbeds, sea aster saltmarsh, brackish and freshwater pools with sand dunes and a shingle beach.

BIRDS A colony of over 40 avocets nests on the enclosed marsh with gadwall, tufted duck, shoveler and black-headed gull, while bearded tit, water rail, bittern and marsh harrier frequent the reedbeds. Common and little terns, ringed plover and oystercatcher nest on the beach where large flocks of waders roost during the highest tides of autumn. During that season many migrants visit the marsh including wigeon, black-tailed godwit, curlew sandpiper and occasional rarities. In winter brent geese and goldeneye occur regularly when divers, grebes and sea duck occur off-shore and snow buntings forage on the beach.

VISITING Access at all times along the west bank to two hides overlooking the marsh and a third hide overlooking the tern colony in summer. The Information Centre is open April to October on all days *except Wednesday*, 10.00am to 5.00pm; otherwise at weekends only. The RSPB Birdshop is open Easter to Christmas all days except Wednesday but weekends and Thursdays only from New Year to Easter, 10.00am to 5.00pm.

FACILITIES

i The Green, Hunstanton, Norfolk (tel: 048 53 2610).

NEAREST RAILWAY STATION King's Lynn with a bus connection to Hunstanton (6 miles).

Lagoons and reedbeds

LOCATION One of a series of nature reserves on the north Norfolk coast, Titchwell is located six miles east of Hunstanton on the A149 road to Brancaster. Enter the reserve car park between Thornham and Titchwell villages. TF/749436.

TENURE 420 acres owned and 90 acres leased from the Crown Estate Commissioners.

STATUS SSSI. Grade 1*. SPA. Ramsar.

WARDEN Norman Sills, Three Horseshoes Cottage, Titchwell, King's Lynn PE31 8BB.

TUDELEY WOODS, KENT

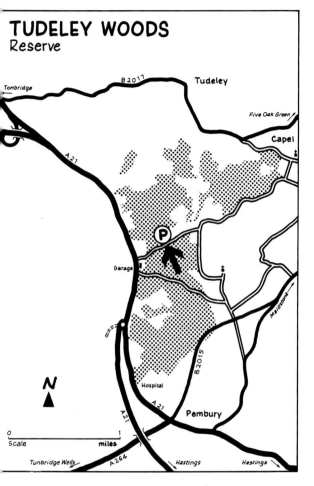

TUDELEY WOODS
Reserve

LOCATION A woodland of the High Weald lying beside the A21 Tonbridge to Hastings road and entered off the minor road to Capel two miles from Tonbridge. TQ/616433.

TENURE 708 acres managed by agreement with the Trustees of the Goldsmid Estate.

WARDEN Martin Allison, 2 Hale Farm Cottages, Hartlake, Tudeley, Tonbridge TN11 0PQ.

HABITAT Deciduous woodland on Tunbridge Wells Sand and Wealden Clay comprising mature oaks with sweet chestnuts and other coppice; also some grazing pasture.

BIRDS Green, great spotted and lesser spotted woodpeckers are common and nuthatches abundant. Blackcap, garden warbler, willow warbler and whitethroat inhabit the coppices. Tree pipit and hawfinch occur annually while hobby, nightjar, crossbill, siskin and long-eared owl may breed occasionally.

OTHER WILDLIFE The springtime carpets of bluebell and primrose can be impressive, and on the sandier soil several scarce heathland species thrive in the rides. Seven species of orchid including greater butterfly, bird's-nest and purple helleborine are found in the woodland.

VISITING Access at all times along two waymarked trails on which visitors are asked to remain.

FACILITIES P

i Town Hall, Tunbridge Wells TN1 1RS (tel: 0892 26121).

NEAREST RAILWAY STATION Tonbridge (3 miles).

Male lesser spotted woodpecker

WEST SEDGEMOOR, SOMERSET

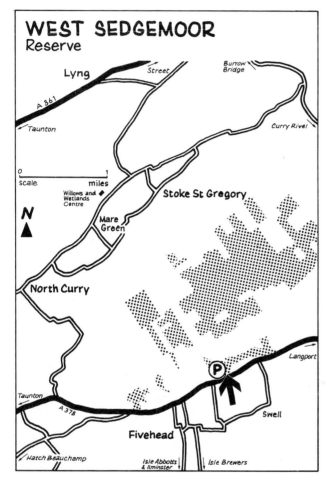

HABITAT Low-lying wet meadows with intervening droves and ditches and bordered by deciduous woodland on the southern scarp. Winter flooding dries in the spring to enable hay-cutting and the subsequent grazing of cattle.

BIRDS Redshank, curlew, snipe, lapwing, black-tailed godwit, yellow wagtail, sedge warbler, whinchat and kestrel nest on the moor where whimbrel are seen regularly on migration. Large flocks of lapwing are joined in winter by golden plover, teal, wigeon and Bewick's swan, depending on the amount of flooding. One of Britain's largest heronries of about 70 pairs is established in Swell Wood, where buzzard, blackcap, marsh tit and nightingales also breed.

OTHER WILDLIFE Marsh marigold, ragged robin and marsh orchid flower in the meadows and water violet in the dykes. Roe deer are often seen.

VISITING Access at all times to the woodland car park, heronry hide and waymarked path with a viewpoint across the moor. There is another hide at the edge of the moor below. The 'Willows and Wetlands' visitors' centre is nearby (see map; tel: 0823 490249).

FACILITIES P & G 30p

i The Library, Corporation Street, Taunton, Somerset (tel: 0823 74785).

NEAREST RAILWAY STATION Taunton (10 miles).

Low-lying meadowland

LOCATION Forming part of the Somerset Levels, this reserve is entered off the A378 road from Taunton to Langport one mile east of Fivehead village. ST/361238.

TENURE 950 acres owned within the much larger moor and extensive scarp woodland.

STATUS Part SSSI. Grade 1.

WARDEN John Leece, 2 Oath Farm Cottages, Burrowbridge, Bridgwater TA7 0JP.

WOLVES WOOD, SUFFOLK

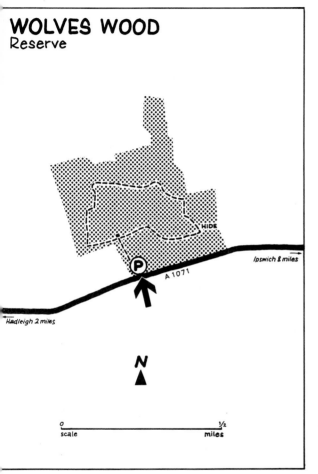

WOLVES WOOD
Reserve

N ▲

```
0          1/2
scale      miles
```

BIRDS Many nightingales favour the scrub and coppiced rides. Other breeding species include garden warbler, blackcap, chiffchaff, willow warbler, nuthatch, great and lesser spotted woodpeckers, marsh and long-tailed tits, woodcock and occasionally hawfinch.

OTHER WILDLIFE Herb paris and yellow archangel indicate this wood's ancient origin.

VISITING Access at all times from the car park around the waymarked trail.

FACILITIES   P   IC   G 30p

  Town Hall, Princes Street, Ipswich, Suffolk (tel: 0473 58070).

NEAREST RAILWAY STATION Ipswich (8 miles).

Female whitethroat

LOCATION This wood lies beside the A1071 road to Ipswich two miles east of Hadleigh, in Suffolk farmland. TM/054436.

TENURE 92 acres owned.

STATUS SSSI. Grade 1.

WARDEN None usually present. Enquiries to Russell Leavett, Stour Wood Reserve (page 65).

HABITAT A mixed deciduous wood of oak, ash, birch, hornbeam, aspen and hazel with an area of coppiced scrub.

RSPB

RESERVES

IN SCOTLAND

BALRANALD, WESTERN ISLES

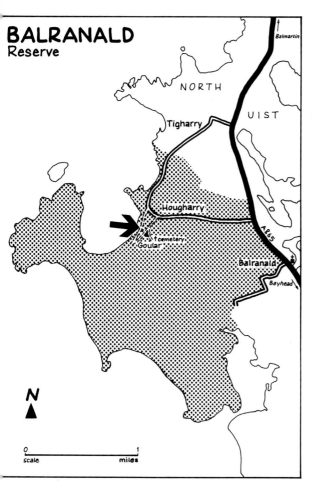

BALRANALD
Reserve

NORTH

UIST

Tigharry

Houngharry

cemetery
Goular

Balmartin

A865

Balranald

Bayhead

N

scale miles
0 1

LOCATION Situated on the Hebridean island of North Uist, the reserve is reached by turning for Hougharry off the A865 road three miles north of Bayhead. The visitor reception cottage is at Goular. NF/706707.

TENURE 1625 acres managed by agreement with three neighbouring estates and the crofting community.

STATUS SSSI. Grade 1.

WARDEN Present from April to August at Goular, near Hougharry, Lochmaddy, North Uist.

Killiecrankie, Tayside

HABITAT Sandy beaches and a rocky foreshore are separated from the machair and marshes by sand dunes and there is a shallow, acidic loch. Most of the reserve is worked as crofting land.

BIRDS One of the last strongholds of the corncrake in Britain. Lapwing, snipe, oystercatcher, ringed plover and dunlin nest (at high densities) on the machair while teal, shoveler, gadwall, wigeon and mute swan nest in the marshes. Other breeding birds include little and Arctic terns, twite, wheatear, eider and black guillemot. Whooper swans, greylags and several raptors visit in winter and there is a considerable passage of birds offshore.

OTHER WILDLIFE Grey seals breed on the offshore island of Causamul. There is an attractive machair flora.

VISITING Access at all times. Visitors are asked to keep to the waymarked paths to avoid disturbing ground-nesting birds.

FACILITIES IC G 30p

i Lochmaddy, Isle of North Uist, Western Isles (tel: 087 63 321).

FERRIES travel daily from Uig on Skye to Lochmaddy or from Oban to Lochboisdale on South Uist. Enquiries to Caledonian MacBrayne, Ferry Terminal, Gourock PA19 1QP (tel: 0475 33755).

Nearby Benbecula is reached by **air** from Glasgow: enquiries to British Airways (tel: 041 332 9666).

Male wheatear

BARON'S HAUGH, STRATHCLYDE

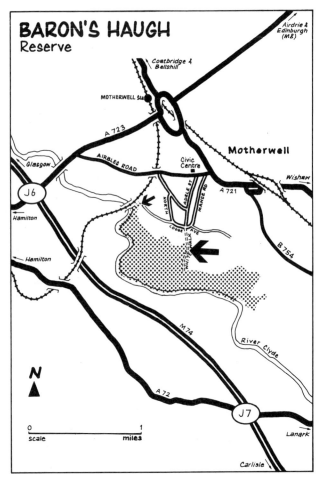

BARON'S HAUGH
Reserve

(Map showing roads and locations: Airdrie & Edinburgh (M8), Coatbridge & Bellshill, Motherwell Sta., A723, Airbles Road, Glasgow, Civic Centre, Motherwell, Wishaw, J6, Hamilton, Hamilton, A721, B754, M74, River Clyde, North Lodge Ave, Whitelaw Walk, Menteith Rd, A72, J7, Lanark, Carlisle, N, scale 0–1 miles)

LOCATION Lying in the Clyde valley one mile south of Motherwell town centre, the reserve is entered via Adele Street opposite Motherwell Civic Centre then by a lane leading off North Lodge Avenue. NS/755552.

TENURE 240 acres owned.

WARDEN Russell Nisbet, 9 Wisteria Lane, Carluke ML8 5TB.

HABITAT Marsh (the haugh) with permanently flooded areas, woodland, scrub, meadows and parkland beside the River Clyde.

BIRDS The haugh attracts wigeon, teal, mallard, pochard and tufted duck in winter as well as over 50 whooper swans. Little grebe, redshank, sedge and grasshopper warblers nest here with kingfisher and common sandpiper along the river. Other breeding birds include garden warbler, whinchat and sparrowhawk.

OTHER WILDLIFE Red squirrels and roe deer occasionally are seen.

VISITING Access at all times. Three hides overlook the haugh (two of which are accessible to wheelchairs) and there is a one-hour walk around it.

FACILITIES P ♿

i The Library, Hamilton Road, Motherwell, Strathclyde (tel: 0698 64414).

NEAREST RAILWAY STATION Motherwell (1½ miles).

Whooper swans on the marsh

BIRSAY MOORS AND COTTASGARTH, ORKNEY

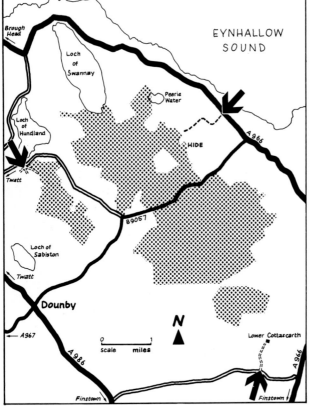

LOCATION Situated in the north of the Mainland of Orkney, this large reserve may be enjoyed from a number of points – see below.

TENURE 3564 acres owned and 2217 acres leased from two owners.

STATUS SSSI. Grade 1.

WARDEN Occasionally present from April to August. Enquiries to RSPB Orkney Officer (page 8).

HABITAT Undulating heather moorland on the Old Red Sandstone with blanket bog, marshy areas and streams.

BIRDS An unusually high density of hen harriers nest here with a few merlins and ground-nesting kestrels. Small colonies of both great and Arctic skuas as well as great and lesser black-backed gulls. Herring and common gulls are also present. Other breeding species include oystercatcher, golden plover, curlew, dunlin, stonechat, wheatear and short-eared owl with several species of ducks.

OTHER WILDLIFE The Orkney vole is common. The Dee of Durkadale is rich in orchids and sedges.

VISITING Access at all times. Cottasgarth is reached along a track by turning left off the A966 road three miles north of Finstown. Just north of Norseman Garage, then right off the minor road at HY/368187. It has a small hide providing good views of the moorland birds, especially hen harriers. A hide by Burgar Hill, by the wind generators, is signposted from the A966 at Evie (HY/358266) and overlooks a red-throated diver breeding site. The Birsay Moors may be viewed from the B9057 road from Dounby to Evie. Dee of Durkadale is reached by turning right along the rough track at the south end of Loch Hundland to the ruined farm of Durkadale (HY/293252). Please close gates.

FACILITIES   **G** to Orkney Reserves 60p

i   Orkney Tourist Board, 6 Broad Street, Kirkwall (tel: 0856 2856).

FERRIES run daily from Scrabster in Caithness to Stromness on Mainland Orkney. Enquiries to P&O Ferries, Orkney and Shetland Services, PO Box 5, Aberdeen AB9 8DL (tel: 0224 572615).

There are **air flights** from Edinburgh, etc. Enquiries to British Airways (tel: 0856 3356) or Loganair (tel: 0856 3457).

COPINSAY, ORKNEY

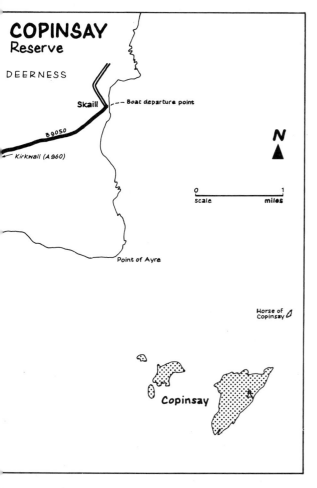

COPINSAY
Reserve

DEERNESS

Skaill --- Boat departure point

B9050

← Kirkwall (A 960)

N ▲

0 scale 1 miles

Point of Ayre

Horse of Copinsay ⌀

Copinsay

LOCATION The James Fisher Memorial island two miles off the east coast of Mainland Orkney near Skaill. HY/610010.

TENURE 375 acres owned.

STATUS SSSI. Grade 2.

WARDEN None present. Enquiries to RSPB Orkney Officer (page 8).

HABITAT An island of Old Red Sandstone with almost a mile of sheer cliffs, also rocky shores connecting it to islets.

BIRDS Very large cliff-nesting colonies of kittiwake, guillemot, razorbill and fulmar with some shags, puffins, black guillemots and cormorants. Both great and lesser black-backed gulls, Arctic tern, rock dove, eider, twite, raven and occasionally corncrake also breed. A good variety of passage migrants can be seen in spring and autumn during periods of easterly winds.

OTHER WILDLIFE There is a fine colony of oyster plant on the beach.

VISITING Access at all times by taking day-trips to the island by boat from Skaill (contact S. Foubister – tel: 085 674 252). Excellent views may be obtained of the cliff-nesting birds from several points but visitors are asked to *take great care*.

FACILITIES **G** to Orkney Reserves 60p

i Orkney Tourist Board, 6 Broad Street, Kirkwall (tel: 0856 2856).

For **ferry** connections see page 78.

Fulmar

CULBIN SANDS, HIGHLAND/GRAMPIAN

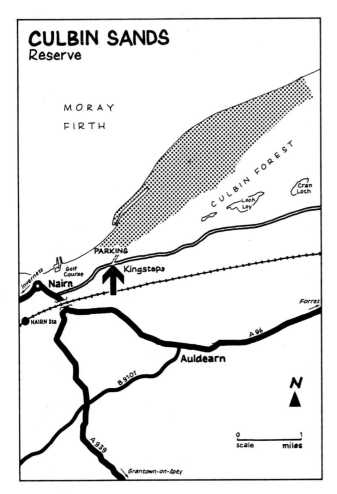

CULBIN SANDS
Reserve

MORAY FIRTH

CULBIN FOREST

Cran Loch

Loch Loy

Inverness

Golf Course

PARKING

Kingsteps

Nairn

NAIRN Sta

Forres

A 96

Auldearn

B 9101

N

A 939

Grantown-on-Spey

scale   miles
0   1

LOCATION On the southern shore of the Moray Firth, this reserve is entered at Kingsteps one mile east of Nairn along the minor road past the golf course. NH/901573.

TENURE 2130 acres leased from two owners.

STATUS SSSI. Grade 1.

WARDEN None present. Enquiries to RSPB Scottish Headquarters (page 8).

HABITAT A long stretch of foreshore comprising sandflats, saltmarsh, shingle bars and spits, backed by the largest sand dune system in Britain, which is almost entirely afforested.

BIRDS Winter flocks of bar-tailed godwit, oystercatcher, knot, dunlin, ringed plover, redshank and curlew with mallard, shelduck, red-breasted merganser and greylag geese. Large concentrations of both common and velvet scoters with long-tailed ducks congregate offshore. Breeding birds include oystercatcher, ringed plover, redshank, a few eider, and little and common terns.

VISITING Access at all times to the beach. Visitors should *beware* of the tides and creeks.

i 62 High Street, Nairn, Highland (tel: 0667 52753).

NEAREST RAILWAY STATION Nairn (1½ miles).

Eiders

FETLAR, SHETLAND

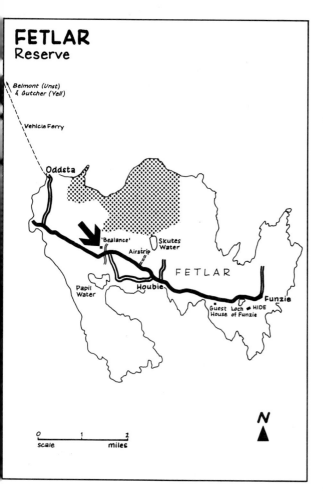

FETLAR Reserve

Belmont (Unst) & Gutcher (Yell)

Vehicle Ferry

Oddsta

'Bealance' Skutes Water

Airstrip

F E T L A R

Papil Water Houbie

Funzie

Guest Loch HIDE
House of Funzie

N

0   1   2
scale   miles

HABITAT Most of the reserve consists of grassy heathland on serpentine rock, encompassing the summits of Vord Hill and Stackaberg, and bordered by high sea cliffs and boulder shores to the north and crofting areas in the south. The heather moor and blanket bog of the west of Fetlar contrasts with some dry heath in the east. Otherwise there are numerous lochs, pools and marshy areas on the island.

BIRDS The reserve is famous for Britain's only pair of snowy owls that nested here from 1969–75, since when only female owls have been resident. Fetlar's breeding birds include Manx shearwater, storm petrel, shag, eider, red-throated diver, golden plover, dunlin, snipe, curlew, raven, twite and an important population of whimbrel. Red-necked phalaropes feeding on the Loch of Funzie (HU/658897) may be watched from the road or a hide. Many passage migrants including rarities occur in spring and autumn.

OTHER WILDLIFE Common and grey seals and otters frequent the coast.

VISITING Visitors are welcome to the island all year, but the reserve and sanctuary may not be entered in summer other than by arrangement with the warden, who escorts parties to view the snowy owls. Bealance is signposted 2½ miles from the Oddsta ferry terminal (HU/604916). Visitors are asked not to disturb the breeding birds and to respect the property of farmers and crofters.

FACILITIES   **G** to Shetland Reserves 50p

i Shetland Tourist Organisation, Market Cross, Lerwick, Shetland (tel: 0595 3434).

Shetland may be reached by **car ferry** from Aberdeen or Orkney or by **air** from Edinburgh, Aberdeen, Inverness and Orkney. Enquiries to British Airways (tel: 031 225 2525). Ferry enquiries to P&O Ferries, Orkney and Shetland Services, PO Box 5, Aberdeen AB9 8DL (tel: 0224 572615).

A **bus** from Lerwick connects with the public ferry but does not cross to Fetlar. Advance booking of vehicles for the ferry is *essential* (tel: 095 782 259/268).

LOCATION Being the smallest of the three inhabited northern islands of Shetland, Fetlar is reached by public car ferry from Yell and Unst. Another ferry connects Yell to the Mainland of Shetland.

TENURE 1700 acres of the northern part of the island is a reserve by agreement with the owners.

STATUS SSSI. Grade 1. A Statutory Bird Sanctuary.

WARDEN Present from April to September at Bealance, Fetlar ZE2 9DJ. Otherwise enquiries to RSPB Shetland Officer (page 8).

FOWLSHEUGH, GRAMPIAN

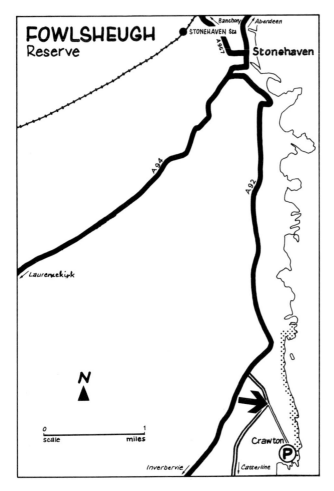

BIRDS Very large colonies of guillemot, razorbill and kittiwake with smaller numbers of fulmar, herring gull, shag and puffin nest on the cliffs. Eiders occur offshore.

OTHER WILDLIFE Seals occasionally are seen.

VISITING Access at all times along the cliff-top path from which the seabirds may be viewed well at several points. Visitors are warned to *take care* at the cliff-edge.

FACILITIES P

i The Square, Stonehaven, Grampian (tel: 0569 62806).

NEAREST RAILWAY STATION Stonehaven (4½ miles).

Guillemots

LOCATION The small cliff-top car park for this reserve is at Crawton which is signposted from the A92 road to Inverbervie three miles south of Stonehaven. NO/876805.

TENURE 1½ miles of cliff owned.

STATUS SSSI. Grade 1*.

WARDEN None present. Enquiries to RSPB Scottish Headquarters (page 8).

HABITAT Old Red Sandstone grass-topped cliffs with nooks and ledges.

HANDA, HIGHLAND

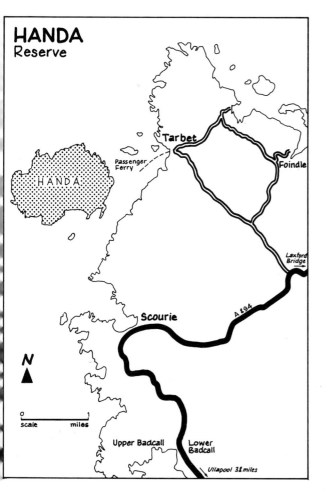

HANDA
Reserve

Tarbet

Passenger Ferry

HANDA

Foindle

Laxford Bridge

Scourie

A894

N

scale   miles
0   1

Upper Badcall   Lower Badcall

Ullapool 38 miles

LOCATION This large island lies off the coast of the Torridon district in the north-west of the Scottish Highlands. It is reached by boat from Tarbet off the A894 road from Laxford Bridge to Scourie. NC/130480.

TENURE 897 acres managed by agreement with the owner, Dr J Balfour.

STATUS SSSI. Grade 2.

WARDEN Present from April to August, c/o Mrs A. Munro, Tarbet, near Lairg IV27 4SS.

HABITAT The island rises from sandy bays to high sandstone cliffs and stacks with an interior of rough pasture, peat bogs and a few lochans.

BIRDS Spectacular numbers of guillemot, razorbill, puffin, kittiwake and fulmar nest on the cliffs with shag and great black-backed gull. Growing colonies of both Arctic and great skuas inhabit the moor with red-throated diver on the lochans, and oystercatcher, ringed plover and eider on the beaches. Many species such as greenshank and whimbrel occur on migration.

OTHER WILDLIFE Various species of whale and dolphin are seen offshore as well as grey seal. Limestone bugle flowers.

VISITING A private boat service to the island operates from Tarbet daily except Sunday between 1 April and 10 September. This service is not connected with the Society which undertakes no responsibility and accepts no liability for the safety of visitors or their property while using it. Visitors undertake the crossing at their own risk and are advised to set out only in calm weather and to take particular care for their own safety during the crossing, as it may be dangerous. Once on the island, visitors are asked to keep to the waymarked path and to *take special care* on the cliff-top from which the seabirds can be viewed well. £1 entry charge for non-members.

RSPB members may stay in the island bothy by arrangement with the RSPB Scottish Headquarters (page 8).

FACILITIES **G** 50p

 Lochinver, Highland (tel: 057 14 330).

NEAREST RAILWAY STATION Lairg (40 miles).

HOBBISTER, ORKNEY

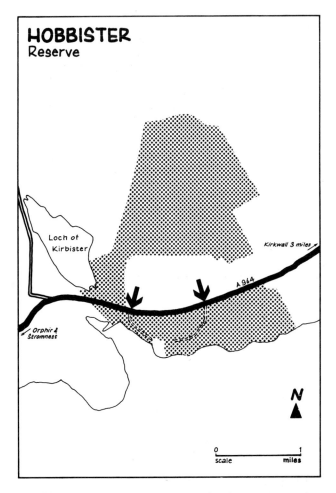

HOBBISTER
Reserve

Loch of
Kirbister

Kirkwall 3 miles

A 964

Orphir &
Stromness

N

0   scale   1   miles

LOCATION Lying either side of the A964 road from Kirkwall to Stromness near the village of Orphir on Orkney Mainland, the reserve may be entered along a track at HY/396070 or a minor road at HY/381068.

TENURE 1875 acres leased from Highland Park Distillery Ltd.

STATUS Part SSSI.

WARDEN Only occasionally present. Enquiries to RSPB Orkney Officer (page 8).

HABITAT Predominantly heather moorland with bogs and fen and drained by the Swartaback Burn. Also low sea-cliffs above the sandy Waulkmill Bay and a small area of saltmarsh.

BIRDS The typical Orkney moorland species of hen harrier, short-eared owl, merlin, red grouse, curlew, snipe, red-throated diver and twite breed on the moorland with colonies of lesser black-backed and common gulls. Fulmar, raven, eider, red-breasted merganser and black guillemot nest on the coast where divers and sea-ducks may be seen at other times.

OTHER WILDLIFE Round-leaved sundew, butterwort and bog asphodel flower in the bogs.

VISITING Access at all times but visitors are asked not to disturb the breeding divers and birds of prey. Waulkmill Bay provides some good birdwatching outside the breeding season.

FACILITIES   **G** to Orkney Reserves 60p

i   Orkney Tourist Board, 6 Broad Street, Kirkwall (tel: 0856 2856).

For **ferry** connections see page 78.

Round-leaved sundew

INSH MARSHES, HIGHLAND

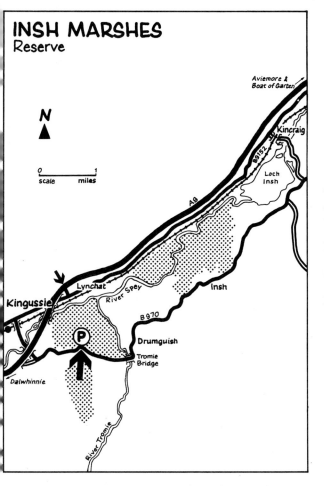

INSH MARSHES
Reserve

HABITAT Extensive marshes in the floodplain of the upper River Spey which usually flood in winter. Also sedge meadows with pools and willow scrub bordered by birch and juniper woodland from which extends some moorland into the foothills of the Cairngorms.

BIRDS The wetland breeding species include wigeon, teal, shoveler, tufted duck, goldeneye, (native) greylag, snipe, curlew, redshank and both sedge and grasshopper warblers. Woodcock, great spotted woodpecker, tree pipit, redstart and occasionally pied flycatcher nest in the woodland with dipper and grey wagtail on the burns. Osprey, hen harrier and buzzard are seen regularly. Large numbers of whooper swans visit the marshes in winter when greylag and pink-footed geese pass on migration.

OTHER WILDLIFE Otter and roe deer are present. Scotch argus is a notable butterfly.

VISITING Open on all days 9.00am to 9.00pm or sunset when earlier. Two hides overlook the marshes and two waymarked trails explore a variety of habitats.

FACILITIES **P IC G** 30p

i King Street, Kingussie, Highland (tel: 054 02 297).

NEAREST RAILWAY STATION Kingussie (1½ miles).

Flooded marshes by the River Spey

LOCATION Situated on Speyside between Kingussie and Loch Insh, the reserve reception and car park is entered off the B970 road to Insh village 1½ miles from Kingussie. NH/775998.

TENURE 1790 acres owned and 315 acres leased from adjacent owners.

STATUS Mostly SSSI. Grade 1.

WARDEN Zul Bhatia, Ivy Cottage, Insh, Kingussie PH21 1NT.

INVERSNAID, CENTRAL

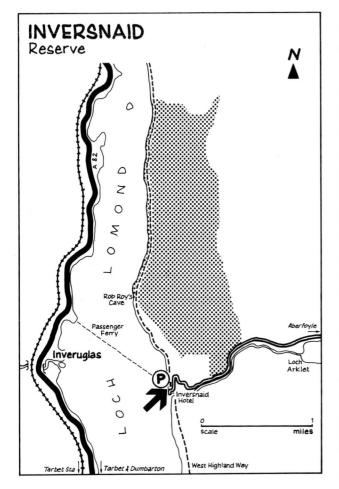

INVERSNAID Reserve

N ▲

LOCATION Lying on the east side of Loch Lomond, this Trossachs reserve is approached by an unclassified road by taking the B829 west from Aberfoyle. NN/337088.

TENURE 923 acres owned.

STATUS Part SSSI. Grade 1.

WARDEN Mike Trubridge, Garrison Cottage, Inversnaid, Aberfoyle FK8 3TU.

HABITAT The ground rises steeply from Loch Lomond through deciduous woodland to a craggy ridge, beyond which lies moorland of grass and heather. Several mountain burns descend to the loch.

BIRDS The resident woodland birds are joined by summer migrants such as wood warbler, redstart, pied flycatcher and tree pipit. Buzzards nest on the crags and in the woods and blackcock frequent the lower slopes. Dipper, grey wagtail and common sandpiper breed on the loch shore and along the burns. The loch itself is a migration route especially for wildfowl and waders.

OTHER WILDLIFE The bryophyte and lichen communities are exceptional. Badger, feral goat and both red and roe deer are present.

VISITING Access at all times along the long-distance footpath, the West Highland Way, which follows the loch shore and offers a pleasant woodland walk. There is a car park at the road end by Inversnaid Hotel where toilets are available during the summer. A pedestrian ferry crosses from Inveruglas on the west bank of Loch Lomond, mainly in summer: telephone Inversnaid Hotel (087 786 223) for arrangements.

FACILITIES P WC

i Main Street, Aberfoyle, Central (tel: 087 72 352).

NEAREST RAILWAY STATION Stirling (35 miles).

View across Loch Lomond

KEN-DEE MARSHES, DUMFRIES AND GALLOWAY

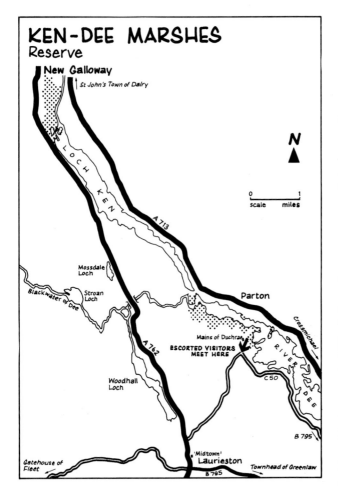

KEN-DEE MARSHES
Reserve

New Galloway
St John's Town of Dalry

LOCH KEN

A 713

Mossdale Loch

Blackwater of Dee

Stroan Loch

Parton

A 762

Mains of Duchrae

ESCORTED VISITORS MEET HERE

C 50

RIVER DEE

Woodhall Loch

B 795

Gatehouse of Fleet

'Midtown'
Laurieston

Townhead of Greenlaw

B 795

N ▲

0 ————— 1
scale   miles

LOCATION Lying in the valley of the River Dee between New Galloway and Castle Douglas, the reserve occurs in two parts beside the river Dee and upstream of Loch Ken.

TENURE 359 acres leased from several owners.

STATUS SSSI. Grade 1.

WARDEN Ray Hawley, Midtown, Laurieston, near Castle Douglas DG7 2PP.

HABITAT Marshes and meadows of the River Dee floodplain bordered by hillside farmland and deciduous woods.

BIRDS In winter some 300 Greenland white-fronted geese visit the valley together with greylag geese, wigeon, pintail, teal, mallard, shoveler, goosander and whooper swans. Hen harriers, peregrines and buzzards hunt the area. The marshland breeding birds include redshank, great crested grebe, teal and shoveler while redstart, pied flycatcher, wood warbler and willow tit nest in the woodland. Crossbills and siskins occur locally.

OTHER WILDLIFE Red squirrels, roe deer and otters are resident.

VISITING There is no access to the reserve other than by *written arrangement* with the warden who escorts parties (charge: £2 to non-members). However, good views of the marshes are obtained from the minor road off the A762 on the west of the valley, as from the A713 on the opposite side. Visitors are asked to park at the roadside *with care* and not to obstruct local traffic.

i Markethill, Castle Douglas, Dumfries and Galloway (tel: 0556 2611).

NEAREST RAILWAY STATION Dumfries which is connected by bus service to Castle Douglas (6 miles).

Hen harrier

KILLIECRANKIE, TAYSIDE

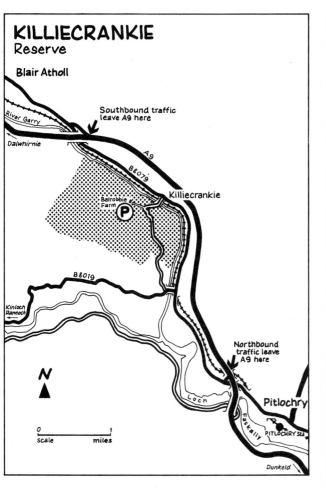

KILLIECRANKIE
Reserve

Blair Atholl

River Garry

Dalwhinnie

Southbound traffic
leave A9 here

A9

B8079

Killiecrankie

Balrobbie
Farm

P

B8019

Kinloch
Rannoch

Northbound
traffic leave
A9 here

Loch

Pitlochry

Fasketly

PITLOCHRY STA.

Dunkeld

N

0   1
scale   miles

LOCATION Lying in Highlands scenery, this reserve is reached by turning off the main A9 road just north of Pitlochry and proceeding to Killiecrankie on the B8079 road, then taking the minor road south-westwards to the warden's house at NN/907627.

TENURE 950 acres leased from J S Murdoch.

STATUS SSSI. Grade 1.

WARDEN Martin Robinson, Balrobbie Farm, Killiecrankie, Pitlochry PH16 5LJ.

HABITAT Sessile oakwoods also containing birch, ash, wych elm and alder rise from the gorge of the River Garry to a plateau of pastureland. Above this a zone of birchwood ascends steeply through crags to a ridge of heather moorland.

BIRDS Wood warbler, redstart, tree pipit and pied flycatcher nest in the woodland as well as garden warbler, crossbill, sparrowhawk, buzzard and both green and great spotted woodpeckers. Black grouse and whinchat frequent the moorland fringe; kestrel, and sometimes raven, inhabit the crags. Both golden eagle and peregrine are seen occasionally.

OTHER WILDLIFE Red squirrels and roe deer are plentiful. A rich reserve flora includes yellow mountain saxifrage, globe flower, grass of Parnassus and several species of orchids.

VISITING Access to the waymarked trails at all times. Visitors may be escorted by written arrangement with the warden (charge: £1 to non-members).

FACILITIES P

i 22 Atholl Road, Pitlochry, Tayside (tel: 0796 2215).

NEAREST RAILWAY STATION Pitlochry (4 miles).

Mixed woodland in the Pass of Killiecrankie

LOCH GARTEN, HIGHLAND

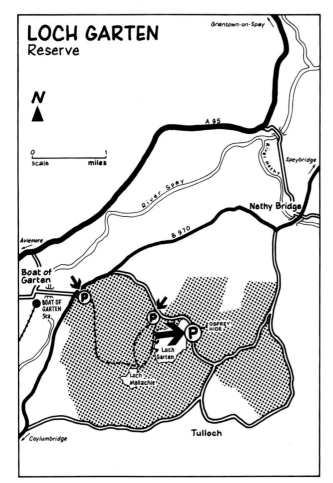

LOCATION Renowned for its osprey observation post, this Speyside reserve comprises a large portion of the Abernethy Forest east of Boat of Garten from which it is signposted off the B970 road to Nethy Bridge. NH/978184.

TENURE 2949 acres owned.

STATUS SSSI. Grade 1*. The osprey nest site is within a Statutory Bird Sanctuary.

WARDEN Stewart Taylor, Grianan, Nethy Bridge PH25 3EF.

HABITAT A very important remnant of the once more extensive Scots pine forest of the Scottish Highlands with an understorey of juniper in places. Also forest bogs, two lochs, some crofting land and a fringe of heather moorland.

BIRDS In addition to the regular nesting pair of ospreys, the reserve has a characteristic breeding birds community of crested tit, Scottish crossbill, capercaillie, black grouse, redstart, siskin and sparrowhawk with teal, wigeon and little grebe on the lochs. Greylag, goldeneye and goosander resort to Loch Garten in winter.

OTHER WILDLIFE The pinewood plants of chickweed wintergreen, bilberry and creeping lady's tresses occur. Resident mammals include red squirrel, pine marten, wildcat and both red and roe deer.

VISITING Provided the ospreys are nesting, the observation post with RSPB shop is open daily from mid-April to August from 10.00am to 8.00pm. Powerful binoculars and telescopes allow close views of the ospreys on their eyrie. Otherwise the reserve is accessible at all times, but visitors are asked to keep to the forest tracks and paths. £1 charge for non-members. Waymarked woodland walks of various lengths can be followed from the two minor car parks. *High fire risk – please do not light fires.*

FACILITIES P IC S ♿ G 50p

ℹ️ Main Road, Aviemore PH22 1PT (tel: 0479 810363). Also tourist information boards in Boat of Garten and Nethy Bridge.

A brief tourist leaflet and comprehensive accommodation register for the immediate area is available from the warden for a large SAE.

NEAREST RAILWAY STATION Aviemore (9 miles). The Strathspey Steam Railway links this to Boat of Garten.

LOCH GRUINART, ISLAY, STRATHCLYDE

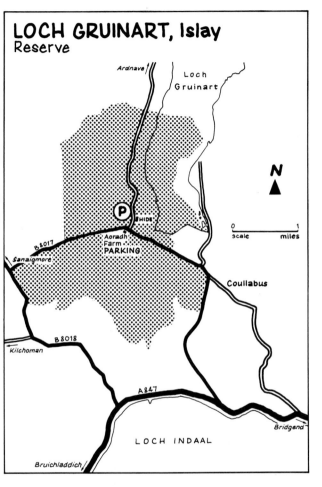

LOCH GRUINART, Islay
Reserve

LOCATION Situated in the north of the Hebridean island of Islay, the reserve lies on the south and west of Loch Gruinart and straddles the B8017 road west of Bridgend.

TENURE 4087 acres owned.

STATUS Partly SSSI. Grade 1*.

WARDEN Mike Peacock, Grainel, Gruinart, Bridgend, Isle of Islay PA44 7PS.

HABITAT Improved and rough pasture 'flats' with saltmarsh at the head of the tidal Loch Gruinart; also moorland with patches of woodland and hill lochs.

BIRDS The major feeding and roosting site in the British Isles for the Greenland race of barnacle geese, numbering up to 20 000 when they overwinter on Islay from October to April. Also large flocks of white-fronted geese. Hen harrier, buzzard and short-eared owl breed and may be seen also in winter with golden eagle, peregrine, merlin, whooper swan and chough. Teal, redshank, snipe, curlew and stonechat nest.

OTHER WILDLIFE Otter, grey and common seals and both red and roe deer are often to be seen.

VISITING Good birdwatching may be obtained from the B8017 and from the hide beside the minor road north to Ardnave. Parking available both here and at Aoradh Farm (NR/276673). Visitors are asked not to enter the fields to avoid disturbing the geese or livestock.

FACILITIES P

i Bowmore, Isle of Islay, Strathclyde (tel: 049 681 254).

FERRIES cross daily from Kennacraig, on Kintyre, to Port Ellen. Enquiries to Caledonian MacBrayne, Ferry Terminal, Gourock PA19 1QP (tel: 0475 33755).

AIR service from Glasgow to Port Ellen. Enquiries to Loganair (tel: 041 889 3181).

Pasture near the loch

LOCH OF KINNORDY, TAYSIDE

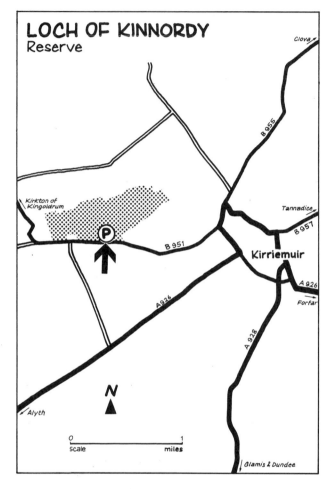

LOCATION Situated off the B951 road one mile west of Kirriemuir. NO/361539.

TENURE 200 acres leased from Lord Lyell.

STATUS SSSI. Grade 2.

WARDEN Present from April to August at The Flat, Kinnordy Home Farm, Kirriemuir DD8 5ER.

HABITAT A freshwater marsh with varying amounts of open water, containing willow and alder scrub, fringed by woodland and set in a farming landscape.

BIRDS Mallard, teal, shoveler, tufted duck, gadwall, great crested and little grebes and ruddy duck nest as well as sedge warbler, reed bunting, redshank and a large colony of black-headed gulls. One or two pairs of black-necked grebes have bred here recently. Sparrowhawk and long-eared owl occur and greenshank, ruff and osprey are often seen on migration. A large roost of greylag geese gathers in winter with a variety of ducks and hunting short-eared owl and hen harrier.

OTHER WILDLIFE The flora includes both northern marsh orchids and mats of bogbean. Northern brown argus and ringlet are two of the butterflies that may be seen, and otters have occurred.

VISITING Open on all days from April to August, and on *Sundays only* from September to November. Hours: 9.00am to 9.00pm or sunset when earlier. The reserve is *closed* from December to March. Paths lead from a small car park to the hides.

FACILITIES P

i Bank Street, Kirriemuir, Tayside (tel: 0575 74097).

NEAREST RAILWAY STATION Dundee (18 miles).

Shoveler drake

LOCH RUTHVEN, HIGHLAND

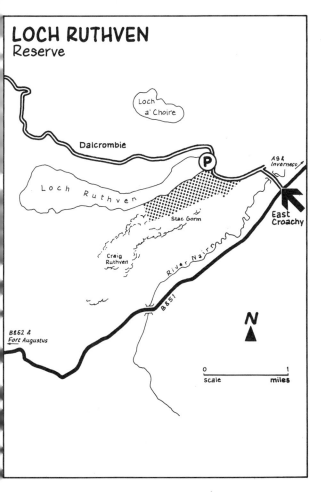

LOCH RUTHVEN
Reserve

Loch a'Choire

Dalcrombie

P

A9 &
Inverness

Loch Ruthven

Stac Gorm

East
Croachy

Craig
Ruthven

River Nairn

B851

B862 &
Fort Augustus

N

0   scale   1   miles

HABITAT Shallow loch shore with sedge beds as well as birchwoods, cliffs and crags and heather moorland.

BIRDS The most important nesting site in Britain for Slavonian grebes. Other breeding birds include red-breasted merganser, mallard, teal, tufted duck, wigeon and coot. The crags attract buzzard, kestrel and raven. Black grouse, ring ouzel, hen harrier and osprey are seen occasionally.

OTHER WILDLIFE Roe deer are present.

VISITING Access at all times from the small car park (*no parking on road please*) to the hide which offers excellent views of the grebes in the breeding season. Otherwise please keep to the waymarked paths to avoid disturbing the grebes.

FACILITIES   P

i 23 Church Street, Inverness IV1 1EZ (tel: 0463 234353).

NEAREST RAILWAY STATION Inverness (11 miles).

Buzzard

LOCATION Situated near Loch Ness to the south of Inverness, the reserve is reached from the A9 via the B851 road to East Croachy, turning north-west along a minor road for one mile. NH/637282.

TENURE 211 acres owned.

STATUS Part SSSI.

WARDEN Present from April to August. Enquiries to RSPB Scottish Headquarters (page 8).

LOCH OF SPIGGIE, SHETLAND

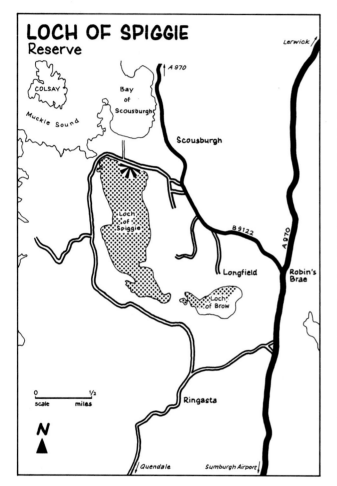

LOCATION Situated near the southern end of Mainland Shetland, the reserve is approached by turning off the B9122 road near Scousburgh which is west of the A970 from Lerwick four miles north of Sumburgh airport.

TENURE 284 acres owned.

STATUS SSSI. Grade 2.

WARDEN None regularly present. Enquiries to RSPB Shetland Officer (page 8).

HABITAT A shallow freshwater loch separated from the sea by sand dunes and from the neighbouring Loch of Brow (partly in the reserve) by a marsh.

BIRDS Teal, shelduck, oystercatcher and curlew nest in the area while the loch is often used for bathing by Arctic terns, both great and Arctic skuas and kittiwakes. Long-tailed ducks gather to display on the loch in spring. As many as 300 whooper swans winter here regularly as well as greylag, tufted duck, pochard, goldeneye and wigeon.

OTHER WILDLIFE Otters are resident.

VISITING The reserve may not be entered, but good views of the loch are obtained from the minor road at the north end HU/373176. Care should be taken not to impede other road-users.

i Shetland Tourist Organisation, Market Cross, Lerwick, Shetland (tel: 0595 3434).

See page 81 for details of **ferries** and **flights** to Shetland. A bus from Lerwick to Sumburgh can disembark passengers at Robin's Brae, two miles from the reserve.

Otter

LOCH OF STRATHBEG, GRAMPIAN

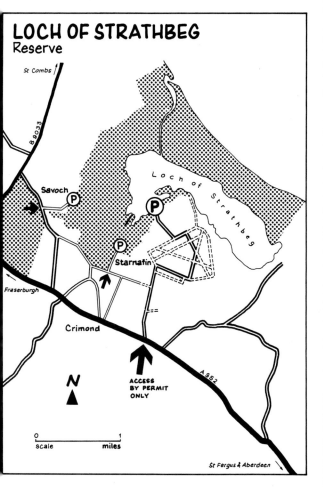

LOCH OF STRATHBEG
Reserve

St Combs

B 8033

Savoch P

Loch of Strathbeg

P

P

Starnafin

Fraserburgh

Crimond

ACCESS
BY PERMIT
ONLY

N

A952

scale   miles

St Fergus & Aberdeen

LOCATION Lying between the sea and the A952 Peterhead to Fraserburgh road near the village of Crimond, the reserve may *only* be entered by permit (see below). NK/063564.

TENURE 441 acres owned and 2000 acres leased from several owners.

STATUS SSSI. Partly Grade 1.

WARDEN Jim Dunbar, The Lythe, Crimonmogate, Lonmay, Fraserburgh AB4 4UB.

HABITAT A large shallow loch on the Aberdeenshire coast, separated from the sea by wide sand dunes and bordered by freshwater fen and marsh, saltmarsh, woodland and farmland.

BIRDS Major concentrations of wintering whooper swan, tufted duck, pochard, goldeneye and both greylag and pink-footed geese gather on and around the loch which also serves as a migratory staging post. There are also red-breasted merganser, goosander, mallard, wigeon and occasionally smew. Breeding birds include eider, shelduck, tufted duck, water rail and sedge warbler. A large colony of Sandwich terns nests on an island in the loch.

OTHER WILDLIFE Roe deer are seen frequently and badgers and otters are present. Lesser butterfly orchids and coral root orchids occur.

VISITING Because access is across MoD property it is *essential* to obtain a permit (charge £1 to non-members) from the warden before visiting the loch. Three hides overlook the bays and islands in the north-west part of the loch and there is a boardwalk through fen woodland from the information centre. However, access is now available at all times to two other parts of the reserve along farm tracks (see map) – no permit or charge.

FACILITIES **P WC IC G** 30p

i Saltoun Square, Fraserburgh, Grampian (tel: 0346 28315).

NEAREST RAILWAY STATION Aberdeen (40 miles).

Tufted duck

LOCHWINNOCH, STRATHCLYDE

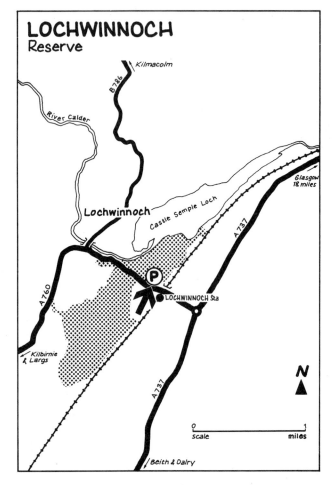

LOCATION The nature centre and reserve lie off the A760 road from Largs to Paisley, ½ mile east of Lochwinnoch. NS/359581.

TENURE 388 acres leased from Strathclyde Regional Council.

STATUS SSSI.

WARDEN John Hawell, Lochwinnoch Nature Centre, Largs Road, Lochwinnoch, Strathclyde (tel: 0505 842663).

HABITAT This reserve comprises the shallow Barr Loch and the sedge marsh of Aird Meadow together with some alder and willow scrub and deciduous woodland.

BIRDS A stronghold of great crested grebes while snipe, shoveler, tufted duck, black-headed gull, sedge and grasshopper warbler also breed. Whimbrel and greenshank occur on autumn passage. In winter whooper swan, greylag, goosander, wigeon, teal, pochard and goldeneye frequent the loch. Kestrel, sparrowhawk and occasionally peregrine may be seen throughout the year.

OTHER WILDLIFE Marsh marigold, yellow water-lily, valerian and both common spotted and greater butterfly orchids flower. Roe deer are seen frequently.

VISITING The reserve is open on all days from 9.00am to 9.00pm or sunset when earlier. The nature trails incorporate four hides overlooking the marsh and open water. The Centre, with observation tower and RSPB gift shop, is open every day *except Thursday* from 10.00am to 5.00pm. Refreshments served at weekends. £1 charge for non-members.

FACILITIES   **P**   **WC**   **IC**   **S**   ♿   **G** 50p

i   Town Hall, Abbey Close, Paisley, Strathclyde (tel: 041 889 0711).

NEAREST RAILWAY STATION Lochwinnoch (immediately opposite the centre).

View from the observation tower

THE LOONS, ORKNEY

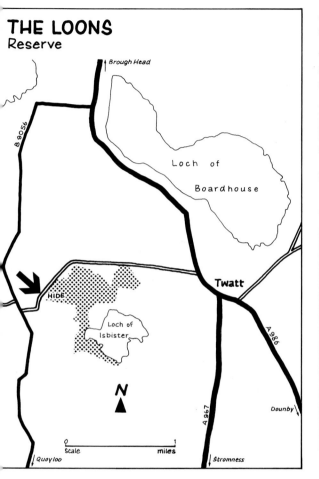

THE LOONS
Reserve

Brough Head

B 9056

Loch of Boardhouse

Twatt

HIDE

Loch of Isbister

A 967

A 986

Dounby

N

Scale   miles

Quoyloo

Stromness

BIRDS Teal, shoveler, wigeon, pintail, red-breasted merganser, snipe and redshank breed here as well as colonies of common and black-headed gulls and Arctic terns. Corncrakes occur occasionally. A regular flock of Greenland white-fronted geese and several species of ducks visit it in winter.

OTHER WILDLIFE Grass of Parnassus, alpine meadow-rue and several species of orchids flower here. Otters occur.

VISITING Access at all times to the hide on the west side (HY/246242) but to avoid disturbance, the reserve itself may not be entered.

FACILITIES **G** to Orkney Reserves 60p

i Orkney Tourist Board, 6 Broad Street, Kirkwall (tel: 0856 2856).

For **ferry** connections see page 78.

Aerial view of the marsh

LOCATION Situated in the north of Mainland Orkney beside the Loch of Isbister, the reserve is approached along the minor road from the A986 three miles north of Dounby.

TENURE 139 acres owned.

STATUS SSSI.

WARDEN None regularly present. Enquiries to RSPB Orkney Officer (page 8).

HABITAT A marsh within a basin of Old Red Sandstone hills, containing old peat workings and bordered by a loch.

97

LUMBISTER, SHETLAND

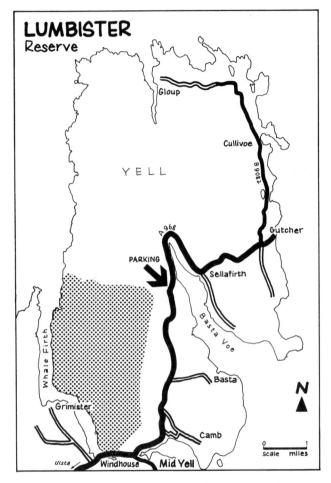

LUMBISTER
Reserve

LOCATION Occupies the west side of the island of Yell between Whale Firth and the A968 road to Gutcher.

TENURE 4000 acres owned.

WARDEN Occasionally present during summer. Enquiries to RSPB Shetland Officer (page 8).

HABITAT Extensive, undulating moorland of heather and bog broken by many water-bodies as well as a steep gorge leading to the rugged grass-topped cliffs and rocky shore of Whale Firth.

BIRDS Red-throated diver, red-breasted merganser and eider nest on the lochs while merlin and both Arctic and great skuas breed on the moorland with golden plover, curlew, dunlin and twite. Raven, wheatear, rock dove, puffin and black guillemot nest on the cliffs.

OTHER WILDLIFE Otters are common and both grey and common seals may be seen off-shore. Lesser twayblades grow in the bogs and juniper and roseroot in the gorge.

VISITING Good views may be obtained from the A968 road. Pedestrian access is gained from the lay-by four miles north of Mid Yell (HU/509974) but visitors are asked to take care not to disturb the divers and other breeding birds.

FACILITIES **G** to Shetland Reserves 50p

_i_ Shetland Tourist Organisation, Market Cross, Lerwick, Shetland (tel: 0595 3434).

A **car ferry** operates between Mainland Shetland and the island of Yell. See also page 81.

Merlin on the moor

MARWICK HEAD, ORKNEY

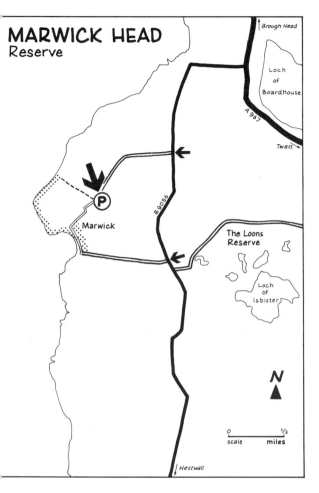

MARWICK HEAD
Reserve

Brough Head

Loch of Boardhouse

A 967

Twatt

P

Marwick

B 9056

The Loons Reserve

Loch of Isbister

N

0   ½
scale   miles

Hestwall

LOCATION Lies on the west coast of Mainland Orkney north of Marwick Bay to which a minor road runs from the B9056. HY/232249.

TENURE One mile of cliffs owned.

STATUS SSSI. Grade 1.

WARDEN None present. Enquiries to RSPB Orkney Officer (page 8).

HABITAT Sheer cliffs of Old Red Sandstone, rising almost to 300ft, on which there are numerous ledges for nesting seabirds. Part of the rocky bay of Marwick and some wet meadowland are also within the reserve.

BIRDS The most spectacular seabird breeding colony on Mainland Orkney, holding very large populations of guillemot and kittiwake. Razorbill, fulmar, rock dove, raven and wheatear also nest here.

OTHER WILDLIFE Thrift, sea campion and spring squill provide a fine show of flowers. Both grey and common seals may be seen.

VISITING Access at all times by walking from the car park at Cumlaquoy (HY/232252), alternatively from the road end at Marwick Bay (HY/229242). The seabirds may be viewed well from the cliff-top, but visitors are cautioned to *take great care*.

FACILITIES   **P**   **G** to Orkney Reserves 60p

i Orkney Tourist Board, 6 Broad Street, Kirkwall (tel: 0856 2856).

For details of **ferries** to Orkney see page 78.

Kittiwakes

MULL OF GALLOWAY, DUMFRIES AND GALLOWAY

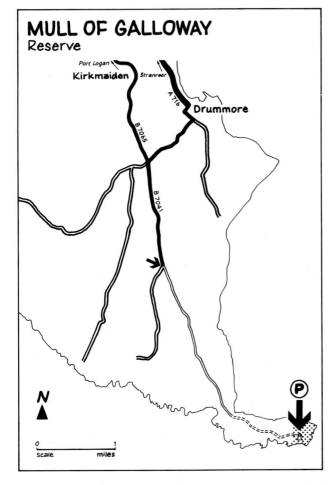

LOCATION Lying at the southern tip of the peninsula south of Stranraer, the reserve is reached via the A716 road to Drummore, then the minor road to the lighthouse and cliffs. NX/157304.

TENURE ¾ mile of cliff is a reserve by agreement with the Commissioners of Northern Lighthouses.

STATUS SSSI. Grade 1.

WARDEN None present. Enquiries to RSPB Scottish Headquarters (page 8).

HABITAT Rugged granite cliffs on the peninsula headland.

BIRDS Nesting colonies of guillemot, razorbill, kittiwake, black guillemot, shag, cormorant, fulmar and both great black-backed and herring gulls. Manx shearwaters and gannets regularly pass the headland.

OTHER WILDLIFE Plants of the cliff-top include spring squill and purple milk vetch.

VISITING Access at all times, but *visitors are warned not to go to the cliff-edge* which is dangerous.

i Port Rodie, Stranraer, Dumfries and Galloway (tel: 0776 2595).

NEAREST RAILWAY STATION Stranraer (21 miles).

Juvenile great black-backed gulls

NORTH HILL, PAPA WESTRAY, ORKNEY

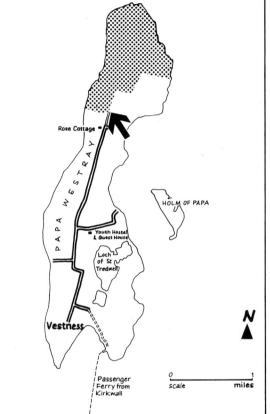

NORTH HILL, Papa Westray
Reserve

Rose Cottage

PAPA WESTRAY

HOLM OF PAPA

Youth Hostel & Guest House

Loch of St Tredwell

Vestness

N

Passenger Ferry from Kirkwall

scale 0 — 1 *miles*

LOCATION The reserve occupies the northern part of this small Orkney island with its entrance at the north end of the principal road. HY/496538.

TENURE 510 acres managed by agreement with the island's crofters.

STATUS SSSI. Grade 1*.

WARDEN Present from mid-April to mid-August, c/o Rose Cottage, Papa Westray KW17 2BU (tel: 085 74 240).

HABITAT A large maritime heath of sedge, heather, crowberry and creeping willow bordered by a rocky coastline with some low sandstone cliffs.

BIRDS An exceptionally large colony of Arctic terns nest on the heath close to Arctic skua, eider, ringed plover, oystercatcher, dunlin, wheatear and four species of gulls. Black guillemot, razorbill, guillemot, puffin, kittiwake, shag and rock dove inhabit the cliffs. Fowl Craig was one of the last great auk breeding sites in Britain. Several migrant species occur including some rarities.

OTHER WILDLIFE Scottish primrose, alpine meadow-rue, mountain everlasting and frog orchid are notable plants.

VISITING Access at all times but visitors are asked to contact the summer warden on arrival, preferably having arranged in advance an escorted tour to view the nesting colonies. These may be viewed well from the perimeter path.

FACILITIES **G** to Orkney Reserves 60p

i Orkney Tourist Board, 6 Broad Street, Kirkwall (tel: 0856 2856).

Contact the Papa Community Co-op, Papa Westray, Orkney (tel: 085 74 267) for details of self-catering and guest house accommodation.

The island is reached by passenger **ferry** from Kirkwall or by **air service** from Kirkwall airport. Enquiries to Loganair (tel: 0856 2494). See also page 78.

Black guillemot

NORTH HOY, ORKNEY

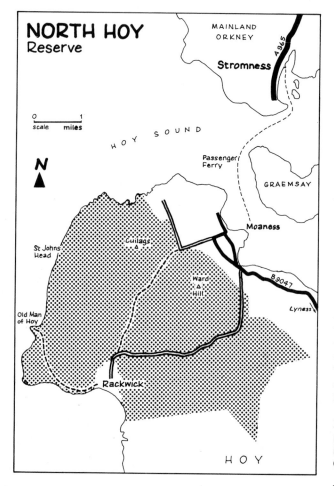

NORTH HOY Reserve

MAINLAND ORKNEY

Stromness

A 965

HOY SOUND

GRAEMSAY

scale miles 0 1

N

Passenger Ferry

Moaness

Cuilags

St Johns Head

Ward Hill

B9047

Lyness

Old Man of Hoy

Rackwick

HOY

LOCATION Occupying the north-west part of the island of Hoy around Ward Hill, the reserve is reached either by passenger ferry from Stromness to Moaness pier then a short walk to the reserve boundary (HY/223034), or by car ferry from Houton to Lyness then up the B9047 road to Rackwick (ND/203995).

TENURE 9700 acres owned.

STATUS SSSI. Grade 1.

WARDEN Keith Fairclough, Ley House, North Hoy, Orkney.

HABITAT A large plateau of moorland, dissected by glacial valleys, and varying from heather and deer grass to mountain heath and sub-Arctic vegetation on the summit. The reserve also contains several miles of spectacular cliffs rising to 1100ft at St John's Head.

BIRDS Large populations of great and Arctic skuas breed on the moorland with red grouse, golden plover, dunlin, curlew, hen harrier, merlin, short-eared owl, twite and great black-backed gull. Guillemot, razorbill, kittiwake, shag, peregrine and raven nest on the cliffs with a colony of Manx shearwaters nearby.

OTHER WILDLIFE Alpine plants such as purple saxifrage, moss campion and Alpine saw-wort grow in the gullies and on ledges. Mountain hares are present.

VISITING Access at all times, there being a footpath through the glen between Ward Hill and Cuilags and another from the village of Rackwick to the famous Old Man of Hoy rock stack. Visitors are warned to *take special care* on the cliff-tops which are crumbly. There is an information display at the Hoy Inn in Moaness.

FACILITIES **IC** **G** to Orkney reserves 60p

i Orkney Tourist Board, 6 Broad Street, Kirkwall (tel: 0856 2856).

Taxis or hire-cars are available on the island – enquire at the pier. See also page 78.

The Old Man of Hoy

NOUP CLIFFS, ORKNEY

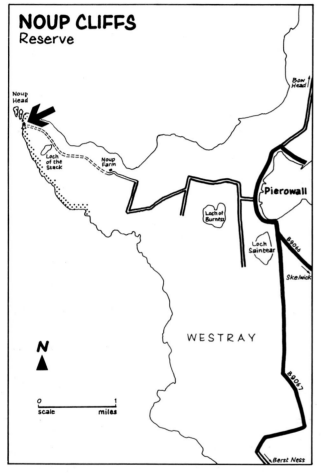

LOCATION Forming the western promontory of the island of Westray, the cliffs are approached from Pierowall along the minor road to Noup Farm then the track to the lighthouse at the north end of the reserve. HY/392500.

TENURE 1½ miles of cliff owned.

STATUS SSSI. Grade 1*.

WARDEN None present. Enquiries to RSPB Orkney Officer (page 8).

HABITAT High sandstone sea cliffs with numerous ledges and backed by maritime heath (off the reserve).

BIRDS This is one of the largest seabird colonies in the British Isles with immense numbers of guillemots and kittiwakes, the other nesting species being razorbill, puffin, shag, fulmar, rock pipit and raven.

OTHER WILDLIFE Grey seals and occasionally porpoises and dolphins are seen off-shore.

VISITING Access at all times to the cliff-top (please *take great care*) from where excellent views may be obtained of the seabirds. Visitors are asked to close gates on the access track.

FACILITIES **G** to Orkney Reserves 60p

i Orkney Tourist Board, 6 Broad Street, Kirkwall (tel: 0856 2856).

The island is reached by passenger **ferry** from Kirkwall or by **air service** from Kirkwall airport. Enquiries to Loganair (tel: 0856 2494). See also page 78.

Grey seal

TRUMLAND, ROUSAY, ORKNEY

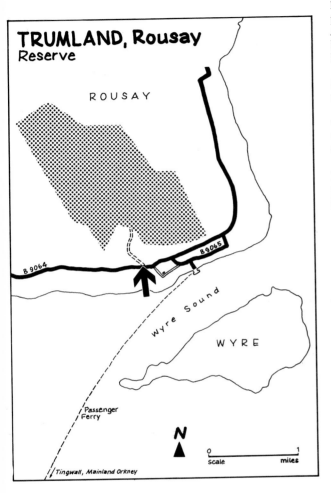

TRUMLAND, Rousay
Reserve

ROUSAY

B 9064

B 9065

Wyre Sound

WYRE

Passenger Ferry

N

0 scale 1 miles

Tingwall, Mainland Orkney

LOCATION The reserve lies above Trumland House in the south of the island of Rousay which is reached by passenger ferry from Tingwall off the A966 road in the north-east of Mainland Orkney. HY/427276.

TENURE 1070 acres owned.

WARDEN Present from April to August at Trumland Mill Cottage, Rousay, Orkney. Otherwise enquiries to RSPB Orkney Officer (page 8).

HABITAT Mainly heather moorland rising to 800ft at Blotchnie Field, dissected by small valleys and containing a lochan and some crags known as 'hamars'.

BIRDS Red-throated diver, hen harrier, kestrel and golden plover breed and short-eared owl, merlin and both great and Arctic skuas may be seen. A mixed colony of herring and lesser black-backed gulls is located on the moorland where both great black-backed and common gulls also nest.

OTHER WILDLIFE Orkney voles are present and otters visit the reserve occasionally.

VISITING Access at all times, but visitors are asked to contact the summer warden who will escort them. A shop and public toilets are located in the village near the pier.

FACILITIES **WC**

i Orkney Tourist Board, 6 Broad Street, Kirkwall (tel: 0856 2856).

For details of **ferries** and **flights** to Orkney see page 78.

Golden plover

VANE FARM, TAYSIDE

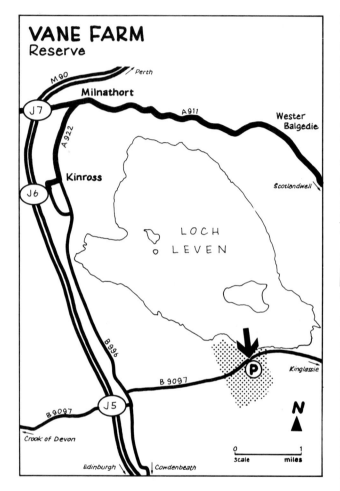

HABITAT A variety of habitats surround this educational nature centre which overlooks Loch Leven: marshy areas with shallow lagoons, mixed farmland and heather moorland with birch and bracken slopes and rocky outcrops.

BIRDS Greylag geese occasionally graze the fields in winter when wigeon, teal, mallard, curlew, shoveler and whooper swan also occur. Large concentrations of pink-footed geese may then be watched over the loch with goosander, tufted duck and pochard. In summer gadwall, shelduck, great crested grebe and redshank frequent the 'scrape' while tree pipit, redpoll and willow warbler occupy the birchwoods.

OTHER WILDLIFE Primrose, wood sorrel, harebell and mountain pansy are some of the plants.

VISITING Access at all times to the car park and nature trail. A hide overlooks the scrape. The nature centre with observation room and RSPB gift shop is open on all days from April to Christmas, 10.00am to 5.00pm, but from 10.00am to 4.00pm January to March. £1 charge for non-members. School parties are especially welcome by appointment.

FACILITIES P WC IC S & G 50p

i Turfhills Service Area, M90, Kinross, Tayside (tel: 0577 63680).

NEAREST RAILWAY STATION Cowdenbeath (8 miles).

View across Loch Leven

LOCATION Lying on the southern shore of Loch Leven east of Kinross, the reserve and nature centre are entered off the B9097 road to Glenrothes two miles east of junction 5 on the M90. NT/160991.

TENURE 298 acres owned.

STATUS SSSI.

WARDEN Jim Stevenson, Vane Farm Nature Centre, Kinross KY13 7LX (tel: 0577 62355).

WOOD OF CREE, DUMFRIES AND GALLOWAY

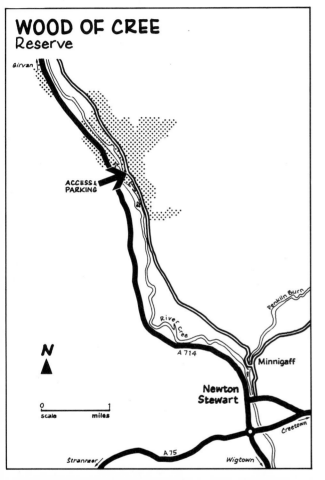

WOOD OF CREE
Reserve

LOCATION Rising from the east bank of the River Cree four miles north-west of Newton Stewart, the reserve is approached on the minor road from Minnigaff running parallel to the A714. NX/382708.

TENURE 659 acres owned.

STATUS SSSI. Grade 2.

WARDEN Paul Collin, Gairland, Old Edinburgh Road, Minnigaff, Newton Stewart DG8 6PL.

HABITAT One of the largest broad-leaved woods in the south of Scotland, consisting largely of old coppice of sessile oak, birch and hazel. Several burns tumble down through the wood from the moorland above to the riverside marsh.

BIRDS Redstart, pied flycatcher, wood warbler, tree pipit, garden warbler, woodcock, great spotted woodpecker, buzzard and sparrowhawk breed in the woods. Common sandpiper, dipper and grey wagtail frequent the streams and mallard, teal and oystercatcher the riverside while curlew and whinchat are found on the moorland fringe.

OTHER WILDLIFE Roe deer and otters are present. Purple hairstreak and dark green fritillary are among the butterflies. There is a rich bryophyte flora.

VISITING Access at all times along a woodland track which leads up from the roadside car parking.

i Dashwood Square, Newton Stewart, Dumfries and Galloway (tel: 0671 2431).

NEAREST RAILWAY STATION Barrhill (14 miles).

Woodcock

RSPB
RESERVES
IN WALES

CWM CLYDACH, WEST GLAMORGAN

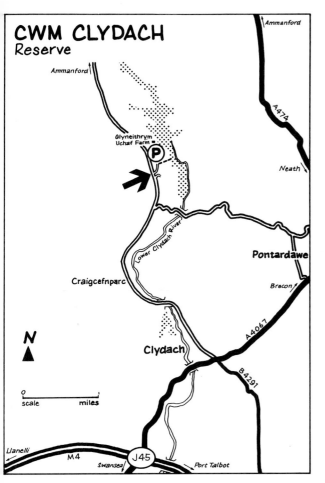

CWM CLYDACH
Reserve

LOCATION Take the minor road up the river valley from Clydach which lies off the A4067 road from Swansea north-east of its junction with the M4. The reserve car park lies three miles north of Clydach, through the village of Craigcefnparc, at Glyneithrym Uchaf Farm. SN/682053.

TENURE 44 acres owned, 22 acres leased and 110 acres managed by agreement with the owners.

WARDEN Martin Humphreys, c/o Ty'n Waun, Craigcefnparc, Clydach, West Glamorgan.

River Tywi, Dinas, Dyfed

HABITAT Oak woodland lining the banks of the lower River Clydach with smaller areas of birch and beech and wetter ground containing ash and alder. Heather and bracken slopes lie above the woodland.

BIRDS Nesting buzzard, sparrowhawk and raven are frequently seen. Nestboxes are used by pied flycatcher, redstart and tits while wood warbler, all three species of woodpecker, nuthatch, treecreeper and tawny owl also nest in the woods. Dipper and grey wagtail frequent the river and tree pipit and wheatear the higher ground. Snipe, woodcock, redpoll and siskin are plentiful in winter.

OTHER WILDLIFE Badger and fox are present. The many species of butterflies include purple hairstreak and silver-washed fritillary.

VISITING Access at all times to a waymarked path along the riverside. Visitors are asked to keep strictly to this footpath and to respect the rights of the farming tenants without whose co-operation the reserve could not have been established.

FACILITIES P

i Singleton Street, Swansea, West Glamorgan (tel: 0792 468321).

NEAREST RAILWAY STATION Swansea (10 miles).

Sparrowhawks

DINAS AND GWENFFRWD, DYFED

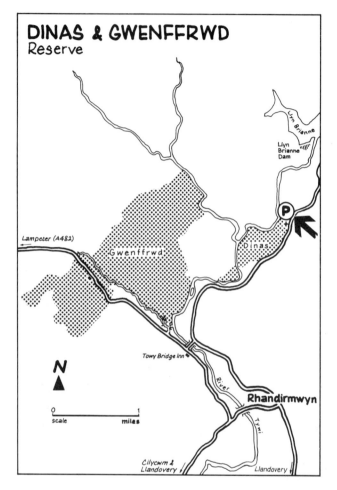

LOCATION Lying in the Tywi valley of the central Welsh hills, Dinas reserve is entered off the road to the Llyn Brianne dam north of Rhandirmwyn village. SN/788472. For access to the Gwenffrwd part of the reserve see below.

TENURE 1723 acres owned.

STATUS SSSI. Grade 1.

WARDEN Tony Pickup, Troedrhiwgelynen, Rhandirmwyn, Llandovery SA20 0PN.

HABITAT Hillside oakwoods with rocky outcrops, streams and bracken slopes rising to heather and grass moorland with valley fields and riverside woodland.

BIRDS Buzzard, sparrowhawk, kestrel, raven and red kite are seen in the neighbourhood, particularly in spring. Many woodland nestboxes are used by pied flycatchers, and other breeding birds include redstart, wood warbler, nuthatch, woodcock, tits and woodpeckers. Grey wagtail, common sandpiper and dipper frequent the rivers, tree pipit and whinchat the hillsides and wheatear and red grouse the moorland.

OTHER WILDLIFE Polecats are seen occasionally. Salmon and trout inhabit the river.

VISITING The Dinas nature trail is accessible at all times from the car park where an Information Centre is open in summer. The terrain is rough and steep in places. For enjoyment of the three-mile hill nature trail at the Gwenffrwd, starting by the warden's house, visitors are asked to report first to the Dinas Information Centre (10.00am to 5.00pm).

FACILITIES **P IC G** 30p

i Central Car Park, Broad Street, Llandovery, Dyfed (tel: 0550 20693).

NEAREST RAILWAY STATION Llandovery (10 miles).

Marsh marigolds by the River Tywi

DYFFRYN WOOD, POWYS

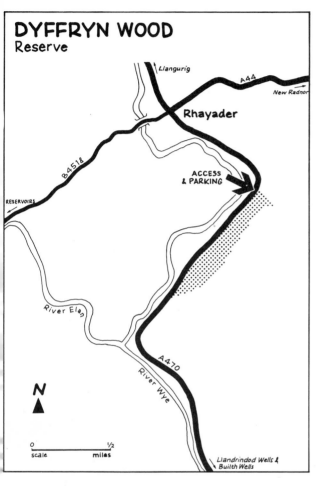

DYFFRYN WOOD
Reserve

BIRDS Pied flycatcher, wood warbler and redstart breed plentifully with a few pairs of raven and buzzard, while grey wagtail and dipper nest along the rocky streams. Whinchat and stonechat frequent the upper woodland fringe where there is the possibility of seeing birds of prey such as peregrine.

OTHER WILDLIFE Badger, polecat, fox and common lizard may be seen. The woodland and ravines are rich in mosses, liverworts and lichens.

VISITING Access at all times to the woodland walk starting at the lay-by at the north end of the wood.

i The Old Swan, West Street, Rhayader, Powys LD6 5AB (tel: 0597 810591).

NEAREST RAILWAY STATION Llandrindod Wells (11 miles).

Polecat

LOCATION Forming part of the composite RSPB reserve holding in the upper reaches of the river Wye and Elan, this wood lies beside the A470 road to Builth Wells just south of Rhayader. SN/980672.

TENURE 65 acres owned and 12 acres managed by agreement with Mr and Mrs Powell.

WARDEN Richard Knight, The Cwm, Llanwrthwl, Llandrindod Wells LD1 6NU.

HABITAT A hillside oak woodland with an area of heather, gorse and bracken and rocky ravines.

GRASSHOLM, DYFED

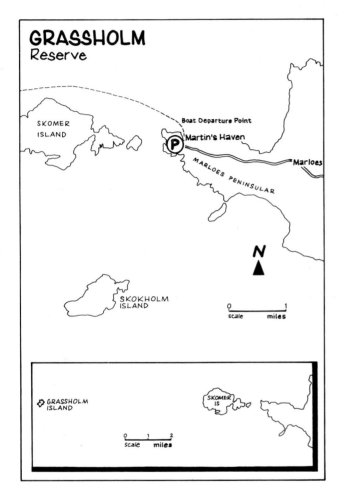

GRASSHOLM
Reserve

SKOMER ISLAND

Boat Departure Point
Martin's Haven

MARLOES PENINSULAR

Marloes

N

SKOKHOLM ISLAND

0   scale   1
         miles

GRASSHOLM ISLAND

SKOMER IS

0   1   2
scale   miles

LOCATION Lies ten miles off the coast of west Wales and beyond the other bird-rich Pembrokeshire islands of Skomer and Skokholm. SM/599093.

TENURE 22 acres owned.

STATUS SSSI. Grade 1*. SPA.

HONORARY WARDEN David Saunders, c/o West Wales Trust for Nature Conservation, 7 Market Street, Haverfordwest, Dyfed (tel: 0437 5462).

HABITAT An isolated, rocky island rising to 150ft above sea level.

BIRDS Grassholm is renowned for its immense breeding colony of gannets numbering over 30 000 pairs, making it the second largest gannetry in the British Isles. There are also small numbers of guillemot, razorbill, shag, kittiwake, herring gull, great black-backed gull and oystercatcher. Manx shearwaters may be seen over the sea.

VISITING The island is inaccessible except in very calm weather. Boat landings are permitted *only from 15 June onwards* so that the gannets are not disturbed while incubating their eggs. There is a boat service from Martin's Haven (SM/761090) on the Marloes peninsula: further details from RSPB Wales Office (page 8). The gannets can be viewed well on the island from outside the sanctuary area which is demarcated by white posts.

i Car Park, Broad Haven, Dyfed (tel: 043 783 412).

NEAREST RAILWAY STATION Milford Haven (12 miles).

Gannets

LAKE VYRNWY, POWYS

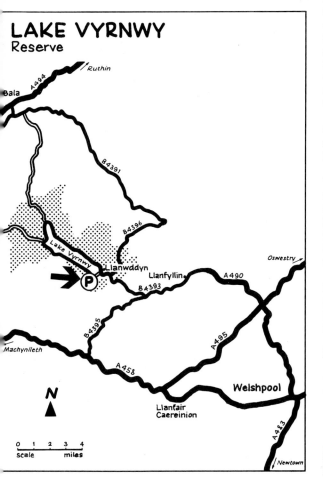

LAKE VYRNWY Reserve

LOCATION This reservoir lies in the Berwyn hills west of Llanfyllin from where the reserve Information Centre by the dam is reached via the B4393 road to Llanwddyn. SJ/020193.

TENURE 1320 acres owned and 16 200 acres of the water catchment managed for conservation by agreement with Severn Trent Water.

STATUS Mostly SSSI. Grade 1.

WARDEN Mike Walker, Bryn Awel, Llanwddyn, Oswestry, Salop.

HABITAT Extensive heather moorland with conifer plantations, mixed deciduous woodland and sessile oakwoods, meadows and rocky streams surrounding Lake Vyrnwy reservoir.

BIRDS Goosander, grey wagtail, common sandpiper, dipper and kingfisher nest by the lake and rocky streams. The mixed deciduous woodland contains nuthatch, treecreeper, sparrowhawk, chiffchaff, garden warbler and both green and great spotted woodpeckers, while the sessile oakwoods are favoured by redstart, wood warbler and pied flycatcher. Crossbill and siskin nest in the conifers. Raven, buzzard, merlin and hen harrier frequent the moorland where wheatear, ring ouzel, curlew and golden plover breed.

OTHER WILDLIFE Red squirrels and polecats are present. The many species of butterflies include pearl-bordered fritillary with large heath on the moorland.

VISITING Visitors may travel round the reservoir by car. There are paths which may be walked, as well as a hide by the north-west shore. Two woodland nature trails, including a hide, are accessible at all times, and there is another hide by the car park which is suitable for wheelchairs. The Information Centre and RSPB Birdshop in the old chapel are open during most hours of the summer, and at weekends over the winter.

FACILITIES P WC IC S & G 50p

i Oswestry Library, Arthur Street, Oswestry, Salop (tel: 0691 662753).

NEAREST RAILWAY STATION Welshpool (21 miles).

Rocky stream near the reservoir

MAWDDACH VALLEY, GWYNEDD

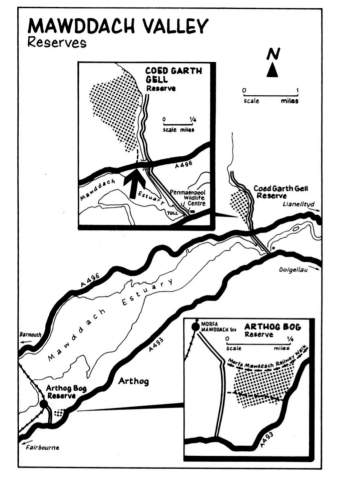

MAWDDACH VALLEY
Reserves

LOCATION Situated in the south of Snowdonia, this composite reserve comprises several properties around the Mawddach estuary. Coed Garth Gell is reached up the public footpath from the A496 Barmouth to Dolgellau Road, starting opposite the Borthwnog Hall Hotel. Arthog Bog may be viewed from the scenic Morfa Mawddach railway walk near the mouth of the estuary.

TENURE Coed Garth Gell: 114 acres owned. Arthog Bog: 12 acres owned.

STATUS Partly SSSI.

WARDEN Reg Thorpe, 2 Tan-y-Garth, Friog, Fairbourne LL38 2RJ.

HABITAT Coed Garth Gell is a hillside sessile oak and birch wood with open areas above a river gorge. Arthog Bog contains willow and alder scrub with pasture beside an extensive raised mire.

BIRDS The breeding birds of Coed Garth Gell include buzzard, raven, pied flycatcher, redstart, wood warbler, tree pipit, lesser spotted woodpecker, grey wagtail and dipper. A few black grouse occur here in winter. Whitethroat, sedge and grasshopper warblers, redpoll and occasionally lesser spotted woodpecker nest at Arthog Bog which water rail visit in winter.

OTHER WILDLIFE Coed Garth Gell is rich in bryophytes and lichens and numbers pearl-bordered and dark green fritillaries among its butterflies. Greater spearwort and marsh cinquefoil occur at Arthog Bog.

VISITING Access at all times to both places. For Coed Garth Gell cars should be parked in the lay-by on the A496 (SH/687191) and for Arthog Bog in the Morfa Mawddach station car park (SH/630138). From late May to September the Penmaenpool Wildlife Centre (see map) is open daily without charge. The railway walk is ideal for wheelchairs.

FACILITIES P IC &

i The Bridge, Dolgellau LL40 1LF (tel: 0341 422888).

NEAREST RAILWAY STATION Coed Garth Gell: Barmouth (7 miles); Arthog Bog: Morfa Mawddach (adjacent).

POINT OF AIR, CLWYD

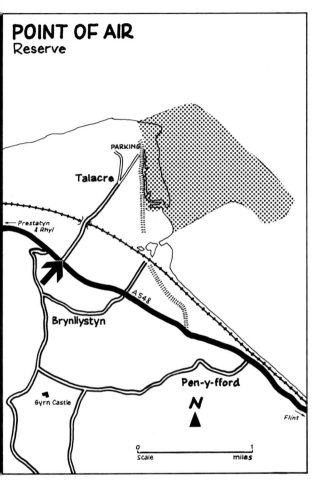

POINT OF AIR
Reserve

Talacre

PARKING

← Prestatyn & Rhyl

A548

Brynllystyn

Pen-y-fford

Gyrn Castle

Flint

N

0 scale 1 miles

LOCATION Lying at the mouth of the Dee estuary on the Welsh side, a vantage point for this reserve is located at the end of Station Road, Talacre, which is reached off the coastal A548 road two miles east of Prestatyn. SJ/113833.

TENURE 600 acres held by agreement with two owners.

STATUS SSSI. Grade 1*. SPA. Ramsar.

WARDEN None present. Enquiries to RSPB Wales Office (page 8).

HABITAT Inter-tidal mudflats with a shingle spit and a small area of saltmarsh.

BIRDS Up to 20 000 waders roost here in winter, particularly oystercatcher, knot, dunlin and redshank, while ringed plover and sanderling occur on migration. Mallard, shelduck, teal, wigeon, pintail and red-breasted merganser also winter when snow bunting, twite and occasionally Lapland bunting and shorelark frequent the shingle spit. Several species of terns occur in summer.

VISITING Access at all times, with limited car parking space on the *landward* side only of the sea-wall. A public hide, situated at the edge of British Coal land and overlooking the Point, is accessible at all times *only* via the sea-wall running south. Visitors are asked not to disturb roosting waders and should not go onto the mudflats when the tide is rising.

i Council Offices, Nant Hall Road, Prestatyn, Clywd (tel: 074 56 2484).

NEAREST RAILWAY STATION Prestatyn (2 miles).

Dunlin

SOUTH STACK CLIFFS, GWYNEDD

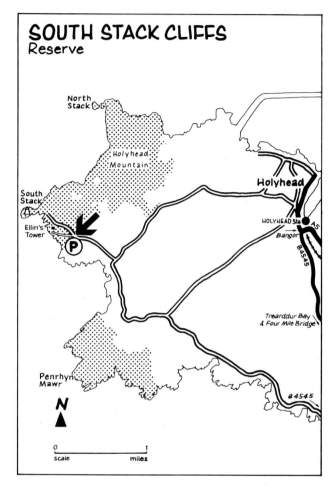

SOUTH STACK CLIFFS
Reserve

North Stack
Holyhead Mountain
South Stack
Ellin's Tower
P
Penrhyn Mawr
N
Holyhead
HOLYHEAD Sta
Bangor
Trearddur Bay & Four Mile Bridge
A5
B4545
B4545

0   scale   1 miles

LOCATION Forming the western headland of Anglesey, the cliffs are signposted by road from both Holyhead and Trearddur Bay. SH/207821.

TENURE 780 acres leased from Anglesey Borough Council.

STATUS SSSI. Grade 1.

WARDEN Alistair Moralee, Swn-y-Môr, South Stack, Holyhead, Gwynedd.

HABITAT High cliffs with caves and off-shore stacks, backed by the maritime heathland of Holyhead Mountain.

BIRDS Several pairs of choughs occupy these cliffs whose ledges are used by thousands of guillemot, razorbill and kittiwake as well as several puffins. Raven, jackdaw, shag and one or two pairs of peregrine also nest here, with stonechat and whitethroat on the heath. Manx shearwaters and gannets pass off-shore and sometimes unusual species like pomarine skua.

OTHER WILDLIFE Silver-studded blue butterflies occur. The cliff-tops are colourful in the spring with thrift and spring squill, and spotted rock rose is a speciality.

VISITING Access at all times to the car park from where a short track leads to Ellin's Tower, the information centre with a panoramic view of the cliffs and seabirds. A closed-circuit television system relays live pictures of the seabirds from April to August. Other car parks are also available.

FACILITIES   P   WC   IC   G 50p

i Marine Square, Salt Island Approach, Holyhead, Gwynedd (tel: 0407 2622).

NEAREST RAILWAY STATION Holyhead (3½ miles).

South Stack Lighthouse

VALLEY LAKES, GWYNEDD

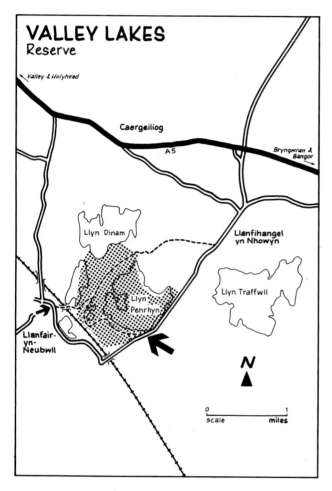

BIRDS Several pairs of great crested and little grebes, ruddy duck, pochard, tufted duck, gadwall, shoveler and mute swan breed here with sedge and reed warblers, stonechat and reed bunting. Numerous shoveler, pochard and ruddy duck are among the wintering wildfowl. Hen harriers and short-eared owls regularly hunt over the reserve when large finch flocks are present in winter.

OTHER WILDLIFE Locally rare plants include cyperus sedge, greater spearwort, flowering rush and marsh fern. There is a good variety of butterflies.

VISITING Although there are no facilities at present, the reserve may be visited at all times via public footpaths which lead from the road at SH/315766 (limited parking here) and SH/305768.

i Marine Square, Salt Island Approach, Holyhead LL65 1DG (tel: 0407 2622).

NEAREST RAILWAY STATION Valley (2 miles).

Pochard drakes

LOCATION Near the north-west coast of Anglesey some two miles south-east of Valley village. SH/310770.

TENURE 150 acres owned.

STATUS SSSI.

WARDEN Alistair Moralee, Swn-y-Môr, South Stack, Holyhead, Gwynedd.

HABITAT The large freshwater lake of Llyn Penrhyn with several smaller reed-fringed pools and areas of fen, grassland and scrub.

YNYS-HIR, DYFED

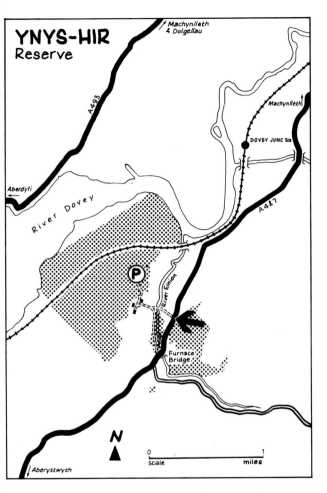

YNYS-HIR Reserve

HABITAT The grazed saltmarsh of the Dyfi estuary is bordered by freshwater marsh and some remnant peat bogs. Mixed deciduous and conifer woodlands, with a river gorge, rise to a rocky hillside with bracken slopes.

BIRDS The oakwoods contain pied flycatcher, redstart, wood warbler, nuthatch and both great spotted and lesser spotted woodpeckers. Goldcrest and coal tit prefer the conifers and sedge and grasshopper warblers the marshland. Buzzard, kestrel and sparrowhawk breed in the woods while red-breasted merganser and common sandpiper frequent the river. Peregrine, merlin and hen harrier hunt over the reserve outside the breeding season. Wintering wildfowl include wigeon, mallard, teal and a small flock of Greenland white-fronted geese.

OTHER WILDLIFE Various sundews, bog rosemary and bog asphodel grow in the bogs. Many butterfly species include dark green fritillary. Badgers and polecats occur.

VISITING Open on all days from 9.00am to 9.00pm or sunset when earlier. A nature trail starts from the information centre, with toilets, and a number of hides are positioned by the estuary and marsh. Another is elevated in the woodland canopy. Charge: £2 to non-members.

FACILITIES **P** **WC** **IC** **G** 50p

 Eastgate, Aberystwyth, Dyfed (tel: 0970 612125).

NEAREST RAILWAY STATION Dovey Junction (3 miles).

Allt-ddu in the Llyfnant valley

LOCATION Lying at the head of the Dyfi estuary, this reserve is entered from the A487 road from Machynlleth to Aberystwyth in the village of Eglwysfach. SN/686956.

TENURE 981 acres owned.

STATUS SSSI. Partly Grade 1. Partly Ramsar.

WARDEN Dick Squires, Cae'r Berllan, Eglwysfach, Machynlleth SY20 8TA.

RSPB
RESERVES
IN NORTHERN
IRELAND

CASTLECALDWELL FOREST, CO FERMANAGH

HABITAT Predominantly a conifer forest fringed by bays of the lough with willow and alder scrub and reedbeds. The reserve also incorporates several low islands in the lough.

BIRDS Of principal importance for the population of common scoters which nest on the vegetated islands with mallard, tufted duck, red-breasted merganser and heron, while common and Sandwich terns use the barer ones. Sparrowhawk, long-eared owl, crossbill and siskin inhabit the forest and both great crested and little grebes the bays. Corncrakes breed in the vicinity. Wigeon, goldeneye, teal, pochard, tufted duck and whooper swan occur in winter.

OTHER WILDLIFE Badger, red squirrel and pine marten inhabit the forest.

VISITING Access at all times to the shoreline paths and a hide in Castle Bay. There is an information centre with toilets. School parties are welcome by appointment. Boat trips can be arranged with the warden.

FACILITIES P IC WC

i Lakeland Visitor Centre, Shore Road, Enniskillen, Co Fermanagh (tel: 0365 23110).

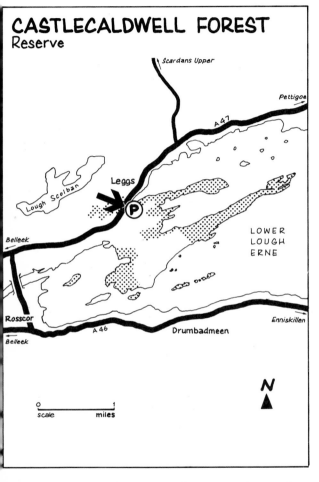

Common terns

LOCATION Lying on the west side of Lower Lough Erne, this peninsula is entered off the A47 road to Pettigoe four miles east of Belleek. H/009603.

TENURE 51 acres of islands owned while 554 acres of the forest are managed by agreement with the Northern Ireland Forest Service.

WARDEN Joe Magee, Castlecaldwell, Leggs PO, Co Fermanagh.

Lower Lough Erne, Castlecaldwell, Co Fermanagh

GREEN ISLAND & GREENCASTLE POINT, CO DOWN

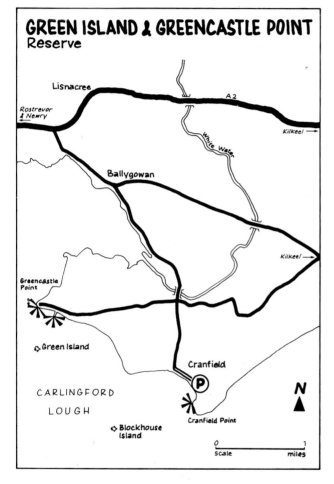

HABITAT Both Greencastle Point and the offshore Green Island (part of the reserve) are small rocky islets.

BIRDS Important breeding colonies of roseate, common, Arctic and Sandwich terns with a few oystercatchers and ringed plovers.

VISITING Good views of the terns may be obtained from the coast road at Greencastle. Access to the islets is strictly *prohibited* to avoid disturbing the nesting birds. Black guillemots nest at the nearby Cranfield Point lighthouse.

i Caravan, Town Centre, Kilkeel, Co Down (tel: 069 37 63092).

Roseate tern

LOCATION A promontory in the north-east of Carlingford Lough five miles south-west of Kilkeel. J/241118.

TENURE 2 acres leased from the National Trust and another owner.

STATUS Green Island is an Area of Scientific Interest.

WARDEN Dave Allen, c/o RSPB Northern Ireland Office (page 8).

LOUGH FOYLE, CO LONDONDERRY

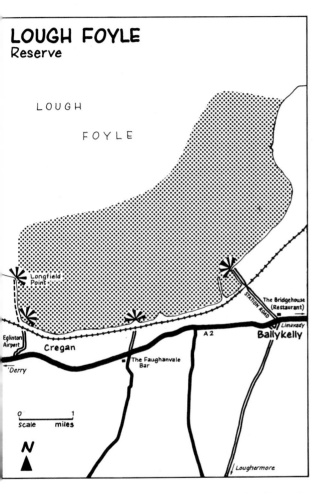

LOUGH FOYLE
Reserve

LOUGH

FOYLE

Longfield
Point

The Bridgehouse
(Restaurant)

Limavady
Ballykelly

Eglinton
Airport

Cregan

'Derry

The Faughanvale
Bar

A 2

STATION ROAD

Loughermore

0   1
scale   miles

N

LOCATION The reserve embraces the south-east foreshore of Lough Foyle from Longfield Point almost to the Roe estuary. C/545237.

TENURE 3300 acres leased from the Crown Estate Commissioners.

STATUS Area of Scientific Interest.

WARDEN Dave Allen, c/o RSPB Northern Ireland Office (page 8).

HABITAT Wide mudflats with a fringe of saltmarsh, shingle and shell ridges bordered by arable farmland (not within the reserve).

BIRDS Lough Foyle is outstanding for its wintering wildfowl including thousands of wigeon, mallard, teal and pale-bellied brent geese with oystercatcher, dunlin, bar-tailed godwit, grey plover and curlew. Up to 2500 whooper swans feed on the adjacent farmland with Bewick's swans and white-fronted geese. Many snow buntings forage on the shore in winter when other unusual visitors include Slavonian grebe and three species of divers. Whimbrel, curlew sandpiper, little stint and spotted redshank are some of the passage migrants.

OTHER WILDLIFE Otters and common seal have been observed here.

VISITING Access at all times to good viewpoints at Longfield Point, Ballykelly and Faughanvale, reached by taking minor roads off the main Limavady–Londonderry road, *taking care at the unmanned railway crossings*. Visitors are asked not to disturb the flocks of waders and wildfowl.

i 7 Connell Street, Limavady, Co Londonderry (tel: 050 472 62226).

NEAREST RAILWAY STATION Londonderry (1 mile).

Mudflats on the lough

RATHLIN ISLAND CLIFFS, CO ANTRIM

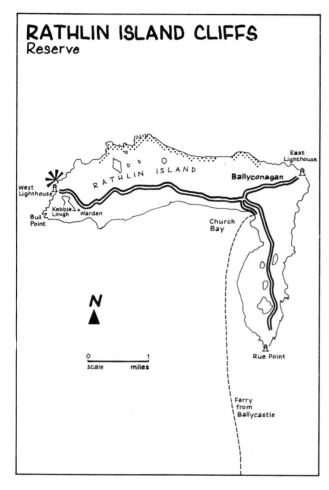

RATHLIN ISLAND CLIFFS
Reserve

HABITAT The RSPB reserve comprises a stretch of basalt cliffs, some high and steep, others with grassy slopes above boulder beaches. The Society also wardens the Kebble Nature Reserve of the Department of Environment (Northern Ireland) which includes seacliffs at the western end of the island.

BIRDS Large numbers of guillemot, razorbill, puffin, black guillemot, fulmar, shag, kittiwake and both great and lesser black-back gulls nest on the Kebble cliffs with stonechat, rock pipit and wheatear in the vicinity. Manx shearwaters nest above the northern cliffs where, as elsewhere on the island, buzzard, peregrine, raven and chough may be encountered. Gannets, skuas and occasionally petrels and sooty shearwaters pass offshore.

OTHER WILDLIFE Limestone bugle, thyme broomrape and several species of orchids flower on the cliffs.

VISITING Access at all times to the cliffs and footpaths. The seabird colony can be viewed well from beside the Kebble lighthouse (D/093516). Auks and shearwaters may be seen during the boat crossing to the island.

 7 Mary Street, Ballycastle, Co Antrim (tel: 026 57 62024).

NEAREST RAILWAY STATION Ballymoney (15 miles). There is an irregular **minibus service** across the island to Kebble.

Raven

LOCATION The island lies five miles across Rathlin Sound and is reached by local boat service from Ballycastle on the north Antrim coast.

TENURE 2½ miles of the island's northern cliffs owned.

STATUS Kebble Nature Reserve is an Area of Scientific Interest.

WARDEN Present from April to August at Kebble, Rathlin Island, Ballycastle, Co Antrim.

SHANES CASTLE, CO ANTRIM

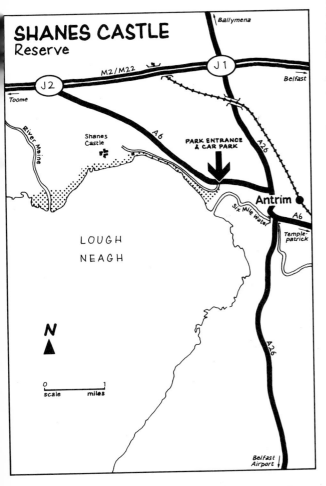

HABITAT Mixed woodland and parkland on the shore of Lough Neagh where there is also some marsh with alder and willow scrub.

BIRDS Heron, kingfisher, great crested grebe, teal, shelduck, long-eared owl, sparrowhawk, blackcap, sedge warbler and magpie nest here. Large flocks of mallard, teal, pochard, tufted duck, goldeneye, coot with some Bewick's and whooper swans, greylag geese and scaup winter on the lough.

OTHER WILDLIFE Red squirrel, badger, otter and fallow deer occur. The plants include heath spotted orchid, adder's tongue and broad-leaved helleborine.

VISITING The reserve is accessible during the times (reviewed each year) when the estate is open to the public, but otherwise by arrangement with the warden. There is a nature trail with a hide overlooking a bay of the lough. The estate operates a steam railway which runs through the park to the Castle as well as a café, toilets and funfair.

FACILITIES P WC

i 43 Queen's Avenue, Magherafelt, Co Londonderry (tel: 0648 32151).

NEAREST RAILWAY STATION Antrim (1 mile).

Red squirrel

LOCATION Forming part of an estate which is open to the public, the reserve lies beside Lough Neagh and is entered from the Randalstown Road one mile from Antrim. J/136874.

TENURE 80 acres leased from the Lord O'Neill.

STATUS Area of Scientific Interest.

WARDEN Eddie Franklin, 67 Greenview Avenue, Antrim, Co Antrim (tel: 084 94 63238).

INDEX TO RESERVES

The Royal Society for the Protection of Birds is *the* charity that takes action for wild birds and the environment. The threats are real – river pollution, the destruction of heathlands, moorlands, hedgerows and estuaries, and illegal shooting, trapping and poisoning of wildlife. The RSPB is fighting these threats, but your support is vital. Birds are everyone's concern. By protecting them we ensure a healthy environment for ourselves and our children. Whatever your age, wherever you live, you can join in the action for birds. Do you enjoy and care about the countryside enough to support us?

—FREE—
RESERVES VISITING
when you join the RSPB

Thanks to the loyal support of over half a million members, the RSPB, the largest conservation charity in Europe, is able to make an effective contribution to the conservation of our wild birds and, even more important, the places where they live.

To continue and expand this important work, we need even more support. You can help us by joining the Society today. In return you will
* have FREE admission to most of our reserves for yourself and one adult living at your address
* receive our popular, full-colour magazine *Birds*, FREE, four times a year
* be eligible to join the countrywide network of Members' Groups
* find an absorbing interest for you and your family

Complete and send the coupon below to:
RSPB, Freepost, The Lodge, Sandy, Bedfordshire SG19 1BR

I would like to help the RSPB in their fight to protect and conserve Britain's birds and countryside.

Please enrol me as a member of the RSPB. I enclose Cheque/PO (payable to RSPB) for £15 (family membership) or debit my Access/Visa Card No._____
(Please quote address of cardholder if different from below) for my first year's subscription.

Expiry date of credit card _____

Cardholder's Signature _____

Mr/Mrs/Miss _____

Address _____

_____

_____ Postcode _____

Send to: **The Royal Society for the Protection of Birds, Freepost, The Lodge, Sandy, Bedfordshire SG19 1BR**